AI Agents

Multiplying Human Potential by Adopting Generative AI

Nils Janse

AI Agents

Multiplying Human Potential by Adopting Generative AI

Nils Janse

ISBN 9798315025214

Contents

Foreword

I remember clearly the day Nils and I first met in Stockholm. We had both been exploring this new strange technology and were astonished by its potential. We were buzzing with excitement, finishing each other's sentences as we brainstormed all the different ways that Generative AI can benefit people, organizations, and the world. We envisioned a future with AI agents working alongside every team, taking care of boring repetitive tasks, assisting in complex workflows, and boosting our productivity in all kinds of ways.

But how do you make it actually happen, as a leader? Where do you start? How do you create a sustainable, systemic change? That's what this book is about. Generative AI is a transformative technology, similar to the Internet. Initially companies struggled to figure out what the Internet was and how to make use of it, but now just about every company uses the Internet in every role and function, and it is hard to imagine a world without it. In this book Nils tackles the crucial leadership challenge: how can you lead a Gen AI transformation across an organization? His five-part transformation model breaks down this complex challenge into clear, manageable pieces that any leader can understand and act on.

This is a practical book. No fluff, just straight to the point. Nils brings together deep expertise across strategy, operations, and technology - all focused on making Gen AI work in the real world. Every day, he's out there in the trenches, working directly with teams and leaders, seeing what works and what doesn't. This book distills those hard-earned insights into clear, actionable guidance.

So congratulations! You've just picked up a truly useful and inspiring book. This is the field guide that every leader needs.

Enjoy the read, and good luck with your AI journey!

- Henrik Kniberg Co-founder Ymnig.ai, author of "Generative AI in a Nutshell"

What If

What if AI's greatest power isn't replacing humans, but multiplying what we can achieve?

Headlines constantly remind us that "AI will replace 40% of jobs." Following this logic, many organizations approach Gen AI as a cost-cutting tool, methodically identifying which roles and tasks can be done by machines instead of people.

Klarna's journey perfectly illustrates the choice organizations face. They began with automation, implementing AI chatbots that cut customer service response times from 11 minutes to just 2. By mid-2024, their CEO announced their AI systems were doing the work of 700 people, with plans to replace 2,000 more.

Yet in February 2025, something fundamental changed. CEO Sebastian Siemiatkowski announced: "We just had an epiphany: in a world of AI nothing will be as valuable as humans!" They realized that automation savings weren't the end goal - they were the foundation for augmenting their people's capabilities to deliver better service where human touch matters most.

This shift represents the two paths organizations can take with Gen AI. The automation path leads to lower costs, improved efficiency, and more streamlined operations - but also creates organizations that are more brittle, less creative, and ultimately vulnerable to competitors who take a different direction.

The augmentation path leads somewhere far more powerful. Every employee becomes dramatically more productive, not by working faster, but by orchestrating a team of AI agents that handle routine tasks, gather information, and help produce better outputs. The organization becomes more adaptive, more innovative, and capable of creating value in ways that weren't possible before.

We're moving rapidly from simple AI chatbots to true AI coworkers that can handle complex tasks independently. But the organizations that truly thrive won't be those that simply replace humans with AI. They'll be the ones that reimagine what's possible when humans and AI work together - where people orchestrate teams of AI coworkers to achieve results neither could accomplish alone.

This isn't a race to automate - it's a race to build new capabilities for human-AI collaboration. The stakes couldn't be higher.

This book shows you how to lead this journey in your organization.

Summary

How can organizations adopt Generative AI and have AI coworkers multiply human capabilities?

This book tries to answer the above question. I'm Nils Janse, co-founder of Ymnig AI, a company that helps organizations adopt Gen AI. Through our work with many organizations on their Gen AI journeys, we've learned what works and what doesn't. We provide training, coaching, and a platform for AI agents, working with everyone from individual teams to entire organizations.

I wrote this book for anyone who wants to help shape how their organization adopts Gen AI. If you're a leader driving organizational transformation, you'll find a clear framework for success. If you're implementing Gen AI across teams, you'll get practical guidance for moving forward. And if you care about building an organization where humans and AI create unprecedented value together, you'll learn how to influence this journey.

Most organizations are in a situation where they know they need to do something about Gen AI, but they're struggling with exactly what and how. Some are stuck in what we call the "wet blanket" phase, where concerns about security and risk lead to policies that effectively prevent any real adoption. Others have given people access to tools like ChatGPT, but aren't seeing the impact they hoped for. Only a few have pushed forward, and they're starting to see dramatic results.

The book is organized in four parts that show you how to build a workplace where humans and AI coworkers create amazing results together:

Part 1: The AI Coworker Revolution

The first part explores how we're moving from today's AI chatbots to true AI coworkers. We'll look at the trends driving this revolution. While current AI chatbots already help people work both faster and better, we're quickly moving toward AI coworkers that can handle complex tasks independently. Soon, every employee will work with multiple AI agents, dramatically multiplying their productivity. Organizations that learn to work effectively with these AI coworkers will have an enormous advantage. Those that do not risk falling behind.

Part 2: Adopting Gen AI By Augmenting People

The second part examines why organizations should focus on augmenting their people with AI capabilities rather than purely pursuing automation, and how this journey typically unfolds through four maturity levels:

1. **Individuals Using Gen AI Chatbots**: People start exploring and integrating AI chatbots into their daily work, discovering personal productivity gains.
2. **Teams Reimagining Work with Gen AI**: Teams systematically examine their processes to uncover potential Gen AI applications, building libraries of reusable prompts.
3. **Introducing Custom Gen AI Agents**: Organizations identify high-value workflows that could benefit from

automation and develop specialized agents to handle them.

4. **Building Joint Human-AI Teams**: Organizations move towards truly integrated teams where humans and AI agents collaborate seamlessly as unified teams.

While these levels show the overall journey, teams don't need to wait for their entire organization to move forward together.

Part 3: Team-Driven Gen AI Adoption

The third part focuses on how individual teams can climb these levels, regardless of where their organization stands overall. It provides practical guidance for teams to build three key capabilities:

1. **Prompt Engineering**: A mini-course on developing effective AI interaction skills, from basic principles to advanced techniques for getting the best results.
2. **Process Re-engineering**: Frameworks and methods for systematically transforming team workflows with Gen AI, including how to identify opportunities and redesign processes.
3. **Agent Implementation**: Step-by-step guidance for developing and deploying custom AI agents, from prototyping to scaling successful implementations.

This team-driven approach creates momentum and builds practical capabilities that can inspire broader organizational transformation.

Part 4: Orchestrating a Gen AI Transformation

The final part examines how to orchestrate the overall Gen AI transformation, focusing on six key drivers:

1. **Urgency**: Building the critical sense of urgency needed to drive action, avoiding excessive caution.
2. **Coalition**: Enlisting a group of leaders and champions who can help drive and support the transformation.
3. **Access**: Quickly enabling safe, broad access to AI tools, and then thoughtfully rolling out agent capabilities.
4. **Learning**: Building both individual and organizational capabilities through structured programs and organic growth.
5. **Strategy**: Developing clear vision and practical steps while maintaining flexibility in a rapidly evolving landscape.
6. **Scale**: Combining strategic orchestration with innovation empowerment and change enablement to drive adoption across your organization.

Through our work with organizations, we've seen these elements help our clients successfully adopt Gen AI. The transformation isn't easy - it requires significant change in how people work and think. But the potential rewards are enormous. Organizations that master working with AI coworkers will create unprecedented value.

The map below shows how the parts of the book fit together - illustrating the journey from individual usage to human-AI teams, the key capabilities teams need to develop, and the six drivers that enable successful transformation.

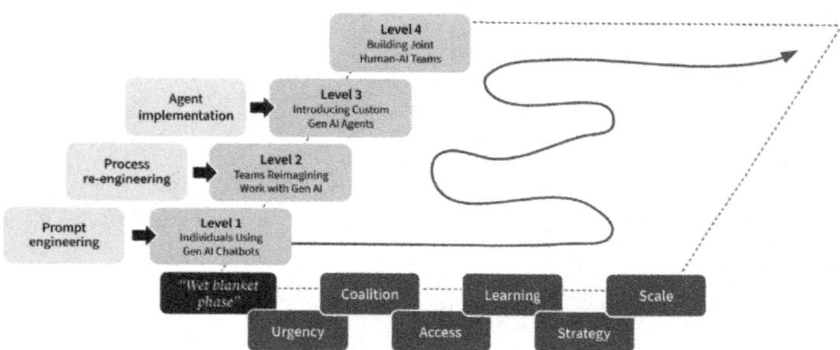

Figure 1. Gen AI transformation journey map

Whether you're just starting your Gen AI journey or looking to accelerate your progress, this book provides both the strategic understanding and practical guidance you need. We'll begin in Part 1 by examining the AI coworker revolution that's transforming how we work, before diving into the practical frameworks, examples, and steps you can apply in your organization.

Part 1: The AI Coworker Revolution

Imagine starting your workday with a team of AI coworkers by your side. These aren't basic AI chatbots - they're capable AI coworkers that can handle almost any task you give them. They work together to get things done, just like a human team would. This change in how we work is already starting, and it will transform the way all of us interact and solve problems.

For example, your email agent will organize your inbox and draft responses to routine messages. Your research agent will gather and analyze the latest industry reports, preparing a briefing for your morning meeting. Your writing agent will collaborate with you on proposals and presentations, the two of you working together to achieve better results than either human or AI could alone. Your meeting agent will record discussions and help draft follow-ups, while your project agent keeps track of your todos, deadlines, and helps you prioritize your work. These AI coworkers will help you with most repeatable work, allowing you focus on strategy, relationships, and creative problem-solving.

In this chapter, we'll explore how we're moving from today's AI chatbots to true AI coworkers. We'll look at the emerging capabilities and the trends driving this revolution. By embracing these new AI coworkers, we can dramatically multiply what each human can accomplish, creating more value than we ever could working alone.

Reflect: Gen AI Impact in Your World
Take a moment to consider these questions:

- How are you already seeing Gen AI change the way people work in your industry?
- What tasks in your daily work could benefit most from having an AI coworker help you?

Your answers will help you connect the concepts we'll explore to your specific context as we look at how AI is evolving from simple chatbots to true AI coworkers.

Gen AI Already Gave Us Powerful AI Chatbots

Let me start by explaining what generative AI actually is. At its core, it's a new type of AI that can create new content - text, images, video, code, and more. One of the main types of Gen AI is large language models, or LLMs. These models work by predicting what word should come next in a sequence. By doing this, they "generate" text, therefore the word "generative" AI, or Gen AI. Before Gen AI came along, using AI meant gathering lots of data and having data scientists build specific models for specific tasks. But recently, the big AI labs have built these massive language models that we can all just use directly.

The first really useful way we got to use these language

models was through AI chatbots like ChatGPT. Even with their limitations, these chatbots turned out to be incredibly versatile. They can help with all sorts of tasks - writing emails and reports, explaining complex topics, and even writing and debugging code. People I work with routinely save several hours per week just by using these basic AI chatbots for their daily tasks.

These early chatbots gave us a glimpse of what's possible. But what we're seeing now is much more interesting - three important development trends that are taking us from simple AI chatbots to true AI coworkers.

The Evolution of Gen AI Capabilities

Let me break down how Gen AI capabilities are evolving through three major development areas shown in the diagram below. Unsupervised pre-training creates fundamental capabilities, providing models with tools enables them to take action, and reinforcement learning makes them more reliable. Together, these advances are creating true AI coworkers.

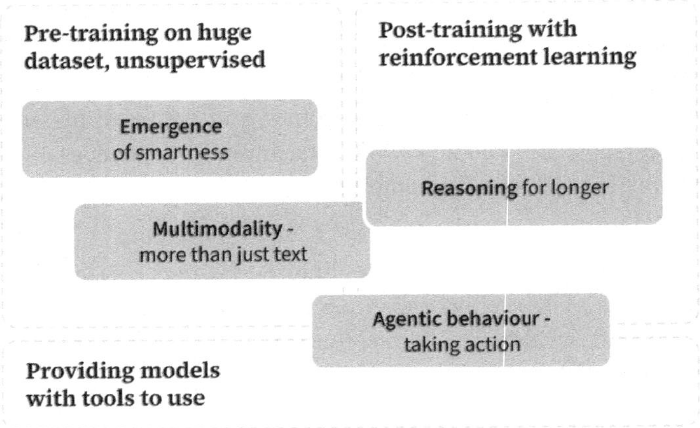

Figure 2. Trends driving Gen AI capabilities

Unsupervised Pre-training on Massive Datasets

The first big development is a fundamental shift in how these AI models are trained. Rather than using supervised learning, where humans need to label data, the big AI labs like OpenAI, Anthropic, and Google DeepMind are now training their models through unsupervised learning on massive amounts of data - basically everything they can find on the internet.

As OpenAI's co-founder Ilya Sutskever famously noted, scaling AI capabilities really only requires two things: unsupervised pre-training and reinforcement learning. This insight has transformed the field. By abandoning the bottleneck of human-labeled data and embracing unsupervised training with increasing computing power, we've unlocked two revolutionary capabilities: emergence and multimodality.

Emergence

What's fascinating about emergence is how these models develop new capabilities just by getting bigger and being trained on more data and for longer. When you build bigger AI models and train them with more compute power, they become smarter in ways we didn't explicitly program - new capabilities "emerge".

Think about how these models evolved: GPT-1 in 2018 could understand basic grammar. By 2022, GPT-3.5 could pass about 10% of the US bar exam. Then GPT-4 came along in 2023 and could pass 90% of the same exam. That's a massive improvement that emerged just from making the model bigger and training it on more data.

Here is an example of what GPT-4 is capable of:

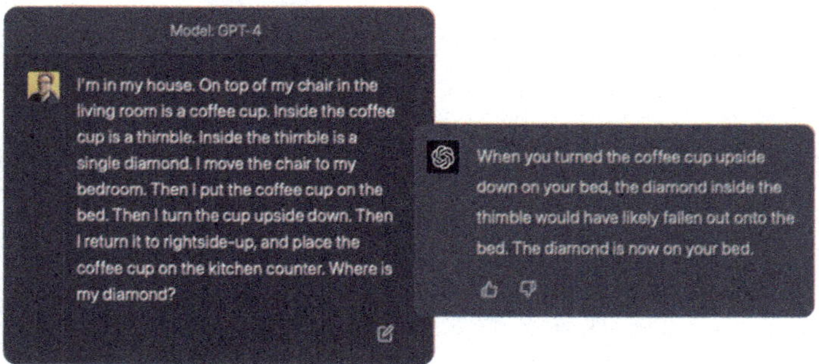

Figure 3. Emergent capability example

It is mind-boggling that these AI models predict just one word at a time. They look at what's written, predict the next word, then the next, and so on. Yet somehow, within this simple word-by-word prediction, they develop an understanding of complex concepts, how objects relate to each other, how physics work, and how to explain things coherently - as shown in the example.

Multimodality

Another wave of capabilities comes from moving beyond just text into multimodality. While early breakthroughs in computer vision relied on supervised learning with labeled datasets like ImageNet, modern multimodal systems now combine these foundations with unsupervised pre-training at scale. By training models on various forms of data - text, images, audio, video, and more - we can create systems that understand and work with many different types of content at once.

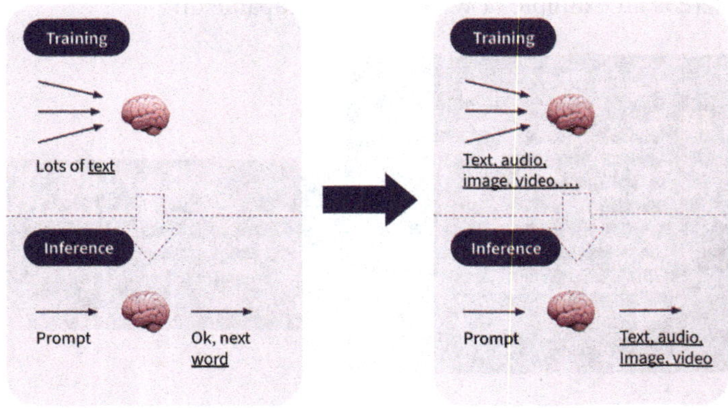

Figure 4. Types of multimodal interactions

For example, GPT-4o, like most advanced LLMs, can now analyze images and create detailed descriptions. Google has a Gemini model that can analyze hour-long videos and understand what happens in them. OpenAI's Sora model was first out to generate realistic videos from text descriptions.

These multimodal capabilities keep expanding - HeyGen has a system where AIs can participate in Zoom calls, showing how these systems are starting to interact in more natural ways.

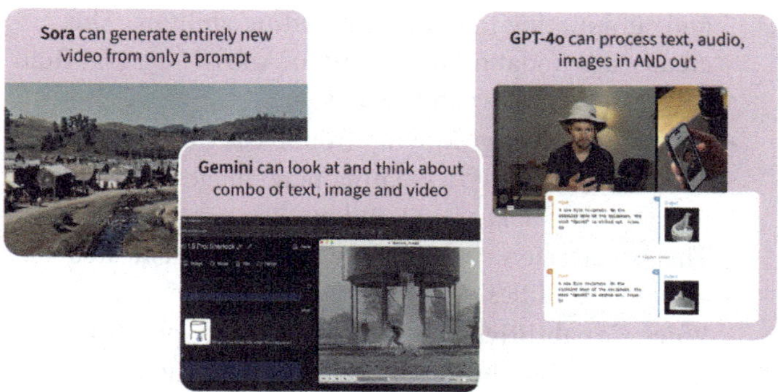

Figure 5. Examples of multimodal capabilities

Providing Models with Tools

When people talk about AI agents, they often get stuck trying to define exactly what makes something an "agent". Even at OpenAI, they reportedly have something like 20 different definitions! I think it's more helpful to talk about "agentic behavior" - to look at the different capabilities that AI systems are developing and how they build on each other.

Here are a few different types of capabilities and a brief explanation of how they can develop to become more powerful:

- **Document Processing & Knowledge**: Starting with basic document reading, AI progresses to finding and combining information from different sources (RAG), and finally develops sophisticated knowledge use where it can understand and apply what it learns across complex information landscapes.

- **Memory & Document Management**: Beginning with conversation memory, advancing to document writing, and culminating in document editing abilities. This creates a foundation for persistent knowledge and fluid collaboration between humans and AI.
- **Image Processing**: Moving from basic image reading and understanding to creating new images, and ultimately being able to edit and modify existing images. This progression enables increasingly sophisticated visual capabilities.
- **Voice Capabilities**: Evolving from basic speech-to-text conversion through text-to-speech generation, and finally to fluid two-way voice conversations. This creates natural, seamless verbal interactions.
- **External Tool Use**: Developing from use of specific adapted tools, to more generally working with different APIs, through to controlling a browser or a computer directly through cursor movement, clicking, and typing - like humans do.
- **Code Management**: Starting with writing pieces of code, then learning to run that code, and ultimately finding and fixing bugs. This creates a powerful feedback loop where AI can improve the code it wrote.
- **Planning & Execution**: Starting with the ability to follow multi-step plans - already a leap beyond basic chatbots that only handle single prompts - progressing to making its own plans, and then iterating on those plans based on results and changing conditions.
- **Event Handling**: Going beyond just being able to respond to chat messages - from reacting to external events like an email or another trigger, evolving to

monitoring systems for potential issues, and on to taking proactive action before problems occur.

- **Self-Improvement**: Progressing from basic error recovery and debugging when faced with obstacles, to analyzing logs and suggesting improvements to its own instructions, and finally to proactively evolving its behavior and capabilities based on accumulated experience without explicit direction.
- **Multi-Agent Coordination**: Advancing from basic agent delegation through agent-to-agent communication, and ultimately to sophisticated orchestration of multiple agents working together.

These capabilities can be visualized as a skill tree, similar to video games where more advanced abilities unlock as foundational skills are mastered:

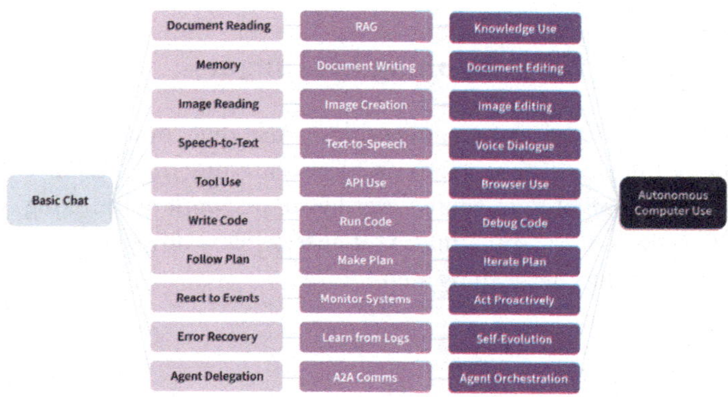

Figure 6. AI Agent Skill Tree

What makes this really powerful is how these capabilities combine. When an AI can use multiple capabilities together - like understanding documents, using tools, and coordinating with other agents - it can handle entire workflows independently. Think about fixing a software bug: the AI could read the bug report, look at the code, try different fixes, and implement the solution that works best, all while coordinating with other agents handling related tasks.

We're moving toward more and more capable AI agents - over time, their capabilities will start to resemble full autonomous use of a computer, like that of a remote human coworker.

Post-training with Reinforcement Learning

While pre-training gives us powerful foundation models, and tools enable agentic behavior, we need something more to make these capabilities reliable enough for real-world use. That's where reinforcement learning comes in.

Reasoning For Longer

The first breakthrough came with models that could take more time to think through problems carefully. It's similar to what Daniel Kahneman describes in his work on thinking "fast and slow" - sometimes you need to slow down and reason things out step by step.

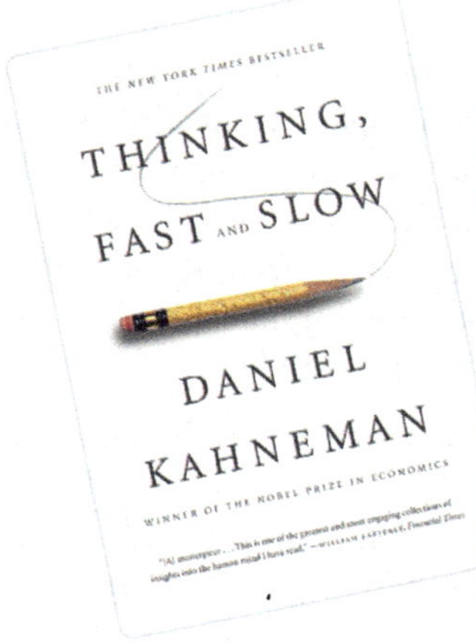

System 1 - Fast

- Automatic thinking system
- Make quick decisions
- Make judgements

System 2 - Slower

- More effortful
- Make deliberate conscious decisions

Figure 7. Two types of thinking systems

OpenAI's o1 model, and its even more capable successor o3, showed that simply giving AIs much more "thinking time" makes them significantly smarter. Instead of rushing to answer, they can carefully consider problems from multiple angles.

And even if thinking for a long time like this only yields the right response one time in a thousand, that can be enough, because then reinforcement learning can be used, and the AI can learn what reasoning worked. This method can largely make up for a lack of training data with long such reasoning chains.

The results have been impressive - o3 has recently achieved a score of over 85% on the ArcAGI benchmark, which is a level that experts thought was years away.

There is a quote by Albert Einstein that goes: "***It's not that I'm so smart, it's just that I stay with problems longer.***" — This is what the models are learning to do now.

Making Agentic Behavior Reliable

Another way in which reinforcement learning becomes valuable is when we combine it with agentic capabilities. Here's why this matters so much: when an AI agent needs to complete an actual meaningful real-world task, it usually requires many steps. Even if the AI is 95% accurate on each step, a 17-step sequence would be very unreliable as errors compound to a horrendous 42% success rate ($0.95^{\wedge}17 \approx 0.42$).

We're already seeing impressive agentic capabilities emerge. For example, Anthropic's Claude model can control computers directly - moving the cursor, clicking buttons, and typing text just like a human would. But these capabilities aren't very useful if they only work sometimes. A 42% success rate for completing multi-step tasks just isn't good enough for real-world use. And there is a lack of data to train on for how to complete a lot of these real-world tasks.

But this is where reinforcement learning comes in. Just like we saw with reasoning, where models can try different approaches and learn from what works, we can apply the same principle to agentic behaviors. Even if an AI only succeeds at a task occasionally at first, reinforcement learning can identify and reinforce the successful patterns. Over time, this drives up the accuracy at each step, pushing the overall success rate closer to 100%. As this process continues, we'll start seeing AI agents that can reliably handle complex workflows by combining multiple capabilities.

Another upcoming frontier is physical robots. I studied mechatronics at university, which in layman's terms means roughly "robot building". The hardest part wasn't building the physical robot - putting all the parts together was pretty straightforward. Instead, it was programming the robot's brain (the computer chip inside) to make the robot move in smart ways. However, now this is changing completely.

Instead of spending months writing complex movement algorithms, we can put an AI model inside the robot and let it learn how to move by itself. For example, Tesla is working on their humanoid robot Optimus, aiming for a 2027 release at a price point similar to a car. While that might be aggressive, it points to where this is heading, and I'd be surprised if we don't see something like it within this decade.

All these capabilities are developing incredibly fast. The AI we're using now is the least capable AI we will ever use. It's only getting more powerful from here.

Looking Further Ahead
For a deeper exploration of where these trends might lead us and what it means for organizations in the longer term, check out the chapter resource on Future Implications of Gen AI, AGI, and ASI.

The Path to AI Coworkers

The trends described above aren't happening in isolation - they're interacting with and amplifying each other. There's an explosion happening in AI-dedicated computing power, better algorithms are being developed by an influx of researchers from physics, math, and other STEM fields, and the chips themselves keep getting better. All of these factors coalesce to create an exponential increase in AI capabilities.

Let me give you an analogy: Imagine going back in time to when mobile text messaging was new. If I stood on stage and showed how I could type a message on one phone and have it appear on another, that would seem amazing. Now think about how that evolved into today's smartphones and everything they can do. In this analogy, ChatGPT is like SMS - we'll look back at it in 10 years and laugh at how basic it was. That's how transformative these trends will be.

We're moving from simple AI chatbots that just answer questions to capable AI coworkers that can handle complex tasks independently. These systems will be able to understand context, take initiative, and work independently toward shared goals - much like remote human coworkers do today.

What if every employee in your organization had several smart, fast, and cheap junior AI colleagues working for them? Think capable AI coworkers that can handle real work. As we saw earlier, these AI coworkers will help with most repeatable work, from managing communications to gathering information and creating content.

But it gets even more interesting when we look at specialized AI coworkers for different business functions:

- *Sales teams* will have AI coworkers handling the time-consuming parts of the sales process. They'll research prospects and prepare detailed briefings before each call. During meetings, they'll take notes and capture action items. After calls, they'll update the CRM, draft follow-up emails, and prepare customized proposals. They'll even monitor customer signals across various channels to identify upsell opportunities and potential issues before they become problems.
- *Marketing teams* will work with AI coworkers that transform their productivity. These agents will monitor competitor activities and market trends, suggesting content topics and campaign ideas. They'll

generate multiple versions of ad copy, social media posts, and email campaigns. They'll continuously analyze campaign performance, run A/B tests, and automatically optimize for better results. They'll handle the tedious work of formatting content for different platforms and ensuring brand consistency.

- *Software development teams* will pair with AI coworkers that accelerate their work significantly. These agents will write initial code implementations and unit tests, spot potential bugs, and suggest optimizations. They'll handle routine code maintenance tasks like updating dependencies and fixing deprecation warnings. They'll keep documentation in sync with code changes, generate API documentation, and help review pull requests for common issues.
- *HR teams* will use AI coworkers throughout the employee lifecycle. These agents will write and optimize job postings, screen resumes against job requirements, and handle initial candidate communications. They'll manage the interview scheduling process, send reminders, and collect feedback. For existing employees, they'll handle routine HR requests, update employee documentation, and even help prepare performance review materials.
- And these are just a few examples - new use cases for AI coworkers are emerging every day as we discover more ways they can help with routine knowledge work.

These AI coworkers will coordinate with humans and each other just like human team members do today. They'll work independently on tasks, share information, and integrate seamlessly into your existing workflows. And because each person and team will work with multiple AI coworkers, they won't just save a couple of hours per week - their productivity will multiply several times over.

Think about that for a minute. At this point, your workforce will become dramatically more productive, with each person effectively orchestrating a team of AI coworkers, and teams getting massive support from AI coworkers that can do all the mundane stuff. The humans will focus on what they do best - strategy, relationships, and creative problem-solving - while their AI coworkers handle the more routine and repetitive tasks that often slow us down today.

Want to learn more about Gen AI?
I won't cover much more on what Gen AI is in this book, only its implications. For a more in-depth description of Gen AI, my colleague Henrik Kniberg has written a great book called "Generative AI in a Nutshell". He explains all the technical concepts in a really simple way, with lots of helpful examples and illustrations. Think of this book as the organizational complement to his more technical guide. Or, if you just want the brief version, you can look at his excellent YouTube video (with the same name).

From Revolution to Augmentation

The AI coworker revolution isn't just coming at some point in the future - it's already beginning. The capabilities we've explored in this chapter are developing rapidly, and organizations that embrace these new AI teammates will gain enormous advantages. But capturing these benefits requires more than just buying some AI tools and hoping for the best.

Through working with many organizations on their Gen AI journeys, I've found that success comes from deliberately building new capabilities in your people. The organizations that thrive are those that help their entire workforce learn to work effectively with AI coworkers.

In the next chapter, we'll explore why augmenting your people with AI capabilities is the key to sustainable transformation, and how to begin this journey. But first, check out the resource chapter that follows - it provides a deeper look at where these AI trends might lead us, including the evolution toward AGI and ASI, and what it means for organizations in the longer term.

Sidebar - Future Implications of Gen AI, AGI, and ASI

While this book focuses on practical guidance for organizations adopting Gen AI today, it's worth considering some longer-term implications. The trends we're seeing with AI agents and coworkers point toward some significant developments that organizations should be aware of as they plan their Gen AI journey.

The Evolution Toward AGI

The capabilities we're seeing emerge in Gen AI today are part of a natural evolution toward what's called Artificial General Intelligence (AGI). This evolution is happening through steady improvements in key areas:

- More structured thinking and reasoning
- Ability to work independently over longer time horizons
- Better spatial and quantitative thinking
- Improved ability to handle different types of information
- More sophisticated agentic behavior

As these capabilities continue to advance, we're moving from today's AI chatbots to AI coworkers, and eventually toward systems that can match or exceed human-level performance across virtually any task - what we call AGI.

This isn't science fiction. The large AI labs are already seeing their models approach human-level performance in many areas. Some labs predict we might see early forms of AGI as soon as 2026-2028. For example, Anthropic's CEO Dario Amodei stated at the 2025 World Economic Forum that "By 2026 or 2027, we will have AI systems that are broadly better than all humans at almost all things." More conservative estimates put AGI in the 2030s. While exact timelines are uncertain, it seems increasingly unlikely that we won't see AGI by 2040.

Beyond AGI lies the possibility of Artificial Super Intelligence (ASI) - AI systems that far exceed human capabilities, potentially becoming as capable as all humans combined. Some experts talk about "takeoff scenarios" between AGI and ASI, with recursive self-improvement, discussing whether this transition might happen quickly (less than a year) or more gradually.

Implications for Work and Skills

This evolution has important implications for how we think about work and skills. The "jagged frontier" concept describes how AI capabilities advance unevenly across different tasks and skills. A helpful mental model for this comes from physicist Max Tegmark - imagine different human skills as islands rising to different elevations above sea level, with advancing AI capabilities like rising water gradually submerging them. Some skill "islands" will remain above water longer than others, but eventually, AI might be able to match or exceed human performance across all domains.

Humans may remain preferred in many roles due to the intrinsic value of human interaction—think of hairdressing, where social experience matters as much as technical skill. Additionally, Baumol's cost disease suggests sectors reliant on personal interaction and inherently slower productivity gains, such as healthcare or education, may become relatively more expensive and prominent in the economy. In many domains, human-AI collaboration, rather than pure automation, will likely define future work, even as AI makes some goods and services essentially free.

Broader Risks and Challenges

While the potential benefits of advanced AI are enormous, we also need to be aware of some significant risks that warrant attention as we navigate this transition:

Existential Risk

As AI systems become more capable, ensuring they remain aligned with human values becomes increasingly crucial. This "alignment problem" represents one of the most profound challenges we face: how do we maintain meaningful control over systems that may eventually surpass human intelligence?

Several promising research avenues offer reasons for cautious optimism. These include advancements in mechanistic interpretability (understanding AI's internal decision processes), chain-of-thought reasoning (making AI thinking more transparent), and developing trust chains where slightly-smarter-than-human AI can help oversee more advanced systems. Additionally, AI systems aren't subject to evolutionary pressures that drive biological survival instincts, potentially making them more amenable to alignment with human values.

The most responsible path forward involves balanced investment - advancing AI capabilities while simultaneously strengthening safety research to ensure these systems remain beneficial partners rather than uncontrollable risks.

Misuse Risk

Even before reaching AGI, there are substantial risks from human misuse of advanced AI systems. These range from enabling creation of dangerous materials to sophisticated disinformation campaigns that could undermine societal trust.

Addressing these challenges requires a multi-faceted approach. While limiting technology spread seems intuitive, it faces practical limitations and may slow beneficial applications. Targeted monitoring of specific high-risk activities (like chemical or biological production) offers a more balanced intervention, though requires careful governance to avoid overreach. Perhaps most promising is the development of "defensive AI" capabilities - tools that help individuals and organizations detect manipulation, verify information authenticity, and build resilience against potential misuse.

By pursuing these protective measures while expanding beneficial AI applications, organizations can help create a technological ecosystem that resists misuse while amplifying positive impacts.

Strain on Democracy

The rapid advancement of AI creates three interrelated societal challenges that could strain democratic institutions.

First, advanced AI may enhance authoritarian control by enabling more sophisticated surveillance and population management. Second, economic concentration may accelerate as organizations with AI advantages capture disproportionate value, potentially widening inequality. Third, labor market disruption could create significant social instability if not managed thoughtfully.

However, these challenges also present a profound opportunity. An AI-empowered citizenry - where broad access to AI capabilities strengthens civil society - could reinforce democratic participation through more informed, coordinated civic engagement.

I am particularly passionate about the survival and strengthening of democracy. This concern is especially close to my heart. The approach outlined throughout this book - augmenting people rather than simply automating their work - has the potential to be part of the solution.

The outcome isn't predetermined - it depends largely on the choices we make as organizations and societies in how we develop and deploy these technologies. Organizations that prioritize augmentation over pure automation can help ensure benefits are widely shared, reducing disruption while building necessary adaptation skills. Democratic institutions themselves could leverage AI to become more responsive while implementing updated social safety nets to manage transition periods.

Strategic Implications for Organizations

These longer-term trends have important implications for how organizations approach Gen AI adoption. The most successful organizations will focus on augmentation rather than pure automation, creating strong human-AI collaboration capabilities. There's a critical path dependency here - companies that rush to automate everything might disrupt their workforce and miss the opportunity to build meaningful human-AI partnerships. Instead, by investing in adaptable skills like complex problem-solving, creative thinking, and relationship building, organizations can keep humans meaningfully in the loop. This approach helps people develop capabilities that will remain valuable even as AI advances, while building a learning culture that continuously evolves as technology changes.

While pursuing their Gen AI journey, organizations should also consider how they can help address the broader risks and challenges I mentioned earlier. This doesn't require a complete shift in focus, but rather an awareness of how their AI adoption strategies might contribute to or mitigate these larger societal concerns. The organizations that will thrive are those that can balance immediate practical action with thoughtful preparation for an AI-enabled future.

Looking Further Ahead

In the very long term, if AI systems become capable of everything humans can do, we might see truly unprecedented levels of abundance - far beyond what we can imagine today. The challenge will be managing the transition period effectively while ensuring the benefits are broadly shared.

This is why the approach outlined in this book - focusing on systematic capability building and human-AI collaboration - is so important. It helps organizations capture immediate benefits while building toward a future where humans and AI can work together effectively, creating more value than either could alone.

Remember though - while it's important to be aware of these longer-term possibilities, the focus should be on practical steps you can take today. The organizations that will thrive are those that can balance immediate action with thoughtful preparation for an AI-enabled future.

Part 2: Adopting Gen AI By Augmenting People

As organizations begin their Gen AI journey, they face a crucial strategic choice that will shape their entire transformation. The most fundamental decision is about people - whether to invest in building your people's capabilities to work with AI, or to primarily implement pre-built AI solutions that automate existing work.

This choice shapes your organization's future. Your approach to Gen AI will determine not just how you implement the technology, but what kind of organization you become.

💭 Reflect: Your Organization's Augmentation Approach

Take a moment to consider these questions:

- To the extent you organization is implementing Gen AI, is it focused more on automating existing processes or augmenting people's capabilities?
- What would it look like if you helped your people become more capable through AI collaboration rather than just automating their work?

Your answers will help you identify your organization's current approach and what might need to change as we explore the maturity levels of Gen AI adoption.

The Strategic Choice: Augmentation vs. Automation

As organizations begin their Gen AI journey, MIT economist Erik Brynjolfsson frames them as facing a choice between two possible futures: In one, we automate away human jobs, gradually cutting people out of the value creation process. In the other, we use AI to enhance human capabilities, giving people "superpowers" that let them create unprecedented value. This choice manifests in two distinct paths:

The **automation path** focuses on implementing pre-built AI solutions to handle existing workflows. This often means partnering with specialized vendors who provide AI tools designed for specific tasks or industries. The emphasis is on quick deployment and immediate efficiency gains. Your people become users of these tools, but aren't deeply involved in shaping how AI is applied to their work.

The **augmentation path** invests in building your people's capabilities to work effectively with AI. Instead of just implementing solutions, you help your people learn to use AI tools creatively, redesign their own workflows, and eventually even create custom AI agents. This approach takes more time and effort, but builds lasting organizational capabilities.

🌍 Real World Example: Leaders Move from Automation to Augmentation

Consider Klarna's journey with Gen AI.
They started firmly on the automation path, implementing AI chatbots that cut customer service response times from 11 to 2 minutes. By mid-2024, their AI systems were doing the work of 700 people, with plans to reduce their workforce by 2,000 more through automation. They seemed to be the perfect example of the automation path. But by early 2025, something fundamental shifted. Their CEO Sebastian Siemiatkowski announced: "We just had an epiphany: in a world of AI nothing will be as valuable as humans!" This marked a strategic pivot toward the augmentation path. They realized that automation savings weren't the end goal - they were the foundation for augmenting their people's capabilities to deliver better service where human touch matters most.

We just had an epiphany: in a world of AI nothing will be as valuable as humans!

Ok you can laugh at us for realizing it so late, but we are going to kick off work to allow Klarna to become the best at offering a human to speak to!!!

So excited about this, more to come!

Last edited 10:44 AM · Feb 14, 2025 · **120.4K** Views

Figure 8. Klarna tweet on value of humans

The long-term business case for augmentation over pure automation is compelling. Organizations that just automate existing processes may see quick wins, but over time they become rigid and vulnerable to change. There's also a people challenge - automation can break the apprenticeship models that organizations rely on to develop expertise. When senior people work primarily with AI rather than junior colleagues, you lose crucial paths for knowledge transfer and skill development. This makes it increasingly difficult to maintain and grow your organization's capabilities over time.

In contrast, organizations that help their employees become more capable through AI collaboration build adaptable workforces that can continuously find new ways to create value. Their employees understand both the capabilities and limitations of their AI coworkers, letting them orchestrate sophisticated workflows that combine the best of human and machine intelligence.

Capturing this potential requires capability building, and building these AI collaboration capabilities takes time and sustained effort. Organizations need to help their people develop an intuition for when and how to work with AI, and this will require significant investment in learning and development.

This doesn't mean automation has no place - many processes can and should be automated. The key is approaching automation as part of a broader strategy focused on augmenting human capabilities. Different parts of your organization might need different approaches. Some areas might benefit from specialized automation solutions, while others need deep investment in human-AI collaboration skills. The goal is finding the right balance that builds lasting organizational capabilities while capturing immediate efficiency gains.

The prize for getting this right is enormous. Imagine an organization where every employee has multiple AI coworkers helping them work more effectively, where teams seamlessly blend human and AI capabilities to achieve unprecedented results. This isn't just about doing existing work faster - it's about fundamentally expanding what's possible. The organizations that invest in building these capabilities now will create workforces that can adapt and thrive as AI technology continues to advance. Their employees will be empowered rather than replaced, using their AI-enhanced capabilities to create more value than ever before.

This book focuses primarily on the augmentation path. While automation has its place, I believe organizations create the most sustainable value by helping their people become more capable through AI collaboration.

It's worth emphasizing that AI typically takes tasks, not entire jobs. While some highly repetitive jobs may be fully automated, in most knowledge work, AI tools allow employees to offload specific tasks while focusing their attention on higher-value activities. Organizations that master Gen AI adoption create workforces with "superhuman productivity" - not by replacing humans, but by enabling them to accomplish far more than was previously possible.

In the sections that follow, we'll explore how organizations can build these capabilities systematically through four levels of maturity.

The Four Maturity Levels of Gen AI Adoption

For organizations pursuing the augmentation path, we typically see progress unfold through four distinct levels of maturity. Each level represents a significant achievement in organizational capability, requiring deliberate effort and investment to reach.

Most organizations start at what we might call "Level 0" - where they might be interested in Gen AI but haven't yet built the capabilities to use it effectively. Many get stuck here, held back by unclear policies or excessive caution. Moving beyond this starting point requires real organizational effort and commitment.

Each subsequent maturity level represents a new plateau of capability that organizations can achieve. Different teams might reach different levels based on their needs and investment in building AI capabilities. What's crucial to understand is that progress between levels isn't automatic - deliberate effort is required to build new skills and develop new ways of working.

Let me outline these four maturity levels:

Level 1: Individuals Using AI Chatbots While it might seem like a small step, achieving this first level is a real achievement - it means your organization has successfully enabled individuals to use Gen AI tools effectively in their daily work. You've overcome initial barriers, established clear policies, and helped people build fundamental AI interaction skills. This creates the foundation for further advancement.

Level 2: Teams Reimagining Work with Gen AI Organizations with teams that achieve this level have helped their teams systematically transform how they work with Gen AI. This represents further progress - teams have moved beyond individual usage to reimagine their collective workflows, create shared practices, and build libraries of proven approaches. Reaching this level requires deliberate investment in team capability building.

Level 3: Introducing Custom AI Agents At this level, organizations have successfully developed and deployed custom AI agents for specific workflows. This is a major advancement requiring an investment - teams must identify high-value opportunities, secure resources, and build the technical capabilities needed for effective agent deployment. Few organizations have reached this level of maturity.

Level 4: Building Human-AI Teams This represents our vision for the highest level of Gen AI maturity - where organizations build truly integrated teams of humans and AI coworkers. While we don't see many examples of this yet, this is where we are headed. Getting there will require deep organizational transformation, sophisticated coordination capabilities, and new ways of structuring work. It's an ambitious target that organizations are just starting to work towards.

In the chapters that follow, we'll explore each of these maturity levels in detail. We'll examine what it takes to reach each level, the capabilities you need to build, and practical approaches for making progress. It's crucial to understand that each level represents real organizational achievement - progress that comes through deliberate effort to build new capabilities in working with AI.

Remember, reaching even Level 1 is an accomplishment. Many organizations struggle to get past Level 0, unable to move beyond initial experimentation. By understanding these maturity levels, you can better plan your organization's journey and invest in the capabilities needed to advance.

Level 1: Individuals Using AI Chatbots

Getting to Level 1 means your organization has succeeded in helping individuals use Gen AI chatbots effectively in their daily work. This is where most organizations start their journey - not with big transformations, but with individual people discovering how Gen AI can help them work better.

Success at Level 1 is relatively straightforward but powerful: everyone using Gen AI chatbots effectively in their daily work. This means people naturally turn to these tools throughout their day, use them confidently for different tasks, and clearly understand what these tools can and can't do well. Some people might use Gen AI ten or more times daily, while others use it less often - but everyone gets clear benefits from it.

Early Adopters Leading the Way

The journey to Level 1 typically starts with early adopters - those people who love trying new tools and solving problems in creative ways. They try out different available tools to see what works best. Often they work in the grey zone of what's formally allowed by company policy. They learn mostly by themselves, sometimes taking online courses they find. They start out small, build confidence by trying things out, and naturally move on to more complex stuff. Over time they start showing others what they've learned.

🌍 Real World Example: Early Adopters Leading the Way

One of my favorite examples of early adopters comes from a large energy company I worked with. A marketing specialist there started experimenting with ChatGPT on her own before any formal AI policy existed. She discovered several use cases that saved her significant time - tasks that used to take hours now took just minutes.

What made her special wasn't just finding value for herself – it was how she shared her discoveries. She posted screenshots of successful prompts on the company's internal chat platform and volunteered to run informal sharing sessions where colleagues could bring work challenges to solve together.

She wasn't especially technical, just someone who enjoyed finding better ways to work. Her LinkedIn posts about practical ChatGPT tips for marketing started attracting attention from peers in other companies too. By the time the company formally explored Gen AI, she had already created a small community of enthusiastic users across departments who were seeing real benefits in their daily work.

The Rest Tags Along

While early adopters do fine with just experimenting, most people need some handholding to get started. They do much better with some structured training to build their confidence. This training doesn't need to be extensive - just enough to help them understand the basics and feel comfortable getting started.

I've now trained over 1,000 people in prompt engineering, and I've learned what really helps people get better at working with AI chatbots. We'll explore these insights and approaches in detail in the Prompt Engineering chapter in Part 3 this book.

As more people start using Gen AI regularly, we see clear patterns emerge. People who use it often save several hours each week on routine tasks, do higher quality work, and even learn new things they couldn't do before. Many also find their work more fun - both because Gen AI helps with boring tasks they didn't like, and because interacting with an AI can be quite stimulating. It should also be noted that some studies indicate people think less critically when they use AI chatbots, so this is something to be aware of, and to instead make an effort to "turn on" the brain.

🌍 Real World Example: Breaking Through Initial Hesitation

At another company we worked with, they ran a company-wide survey about Gen AI usage after six months of having ChatGPT available to everyone. The results showed a clear split in adoption – some were power users, using it 10+ times daily. But most were using it just 2-4 times per week, and a sizeable group reported using it only once or not at all.

When we investigated, we found most people weren't resistant – they just didn't feel confident about using it effectively. One person told me, "I tried it a couple times and got okay results, but I wasn't sure if I was doing it right."

The company ran a series of role-specific workshops teaching basic prompt engineering. Within a month, the number of daily users more than doubled. Even the power users reported significant benefits. One told me, "I was already using ChatGPT constantly, but learning better prompting techniques has saved me another hour each day."

From Individual Users to Team Adoption

As more individuals become regular Gen AI users and understand what these tools can do, organizations become ready for Level 2. This next level is about moving beyond ad hoc individual usage to systematically looking at how teams can transform their processes with Gen AI. While early adopters sharing their experiences can help spark ideas, the real work is in teams deliberately analyzing their workflows and finding ways to improve them together using Gen AI.

In the next chapter, we'll explore what happens when teams start collaborating on transforming their processes with Gen AI.

Level 2: Teams Reimagining Work with Gen AI

While Level 1 focuses on individual adoption of Gen AI chatbots, Level 2 represents a real achievement in team-level transformation. This progress doesn't happen automatically - it requires deliberate effort to move beyond ad-hoc individual usage to systematic team-wide implementation.

Success at Level 2 means teams have systematically examined their core processes to find valuable Gen AI applications - not just the obvious ones that individuals naturally discover, but also some of the less obvious opportunities that emerge from a structured analysis. Teams maintain libraries of reusable prompts, consistently apply best practices, and have a process in place to regularly re-evaluate their ways of working as Gen AI capabilities continue to evolve.

We Need to Recalibrate

Figure 9. Kent Beck: I need to recalibrate

There is this tweet by programming guru Kent Beck that really struck me. He wrote about trying ChatGPT for the first time: "The value of 90% of my skills just dropped to $0. The leverage for the remaining 10% went up 1000x. I need to recalibrate."

I think this tweet really captures what many of us are facing. We've spent years building up our skills and expertise, and suddenly Gen AI comes along and changes everything. For example, I've spent many years as a management consultant and board member, learning how to write structured business memos - I used to think the actual writing was a really powerful skill, but that's something the latest models can now do in seconds. What's become more valuable isn't the writing itself, but the strategic thinking behind these memos. I can now create and iterate on memos much faster, which means the quality of my thinking and analysis matters even more. Some of what we do can now be done by AI in seconds. But that's not the whole story - it actually makes some of our deeper skills, like our experience, critical thinking and creative problem-solving, way more valuable. By using those skills together with the AI, we can reach further faster. So just like Kent on coding and me on business memos, we all need to figure out which of our skills still matter, and how to use AI to amplify them.

Process Re-engineering

Before diving into process re-engineering, a common question is: when should a team make this move? While some teams jump straight in after basic prompt engineering training, I've found it usually works better to give teams a few weeks to practice and internalize their prompt engineering skills first. The key signal is when team members are regularly reusing the same prompts for valuable use cases - that's when it makes sense to take a more systematic approach to process transformation.

This systematic approach builds on what teams have learned through individual usage. Process re-engineering, a methodology that management consultants have used for decades, is making a comeback with a Gen AI twist. While the most ambitious form involves completely reimagining ways of working, the immediate focus is often more practical: methodically examining every task and workflow to identify Gen AI opportunities.

Teams need structured methods to analyze their current processes, identify potential Gen AI applications, and implement improvements. This isn't just about finding obvious use cases - it's about turning over every stone to discover all the places where Gen AI could add value.

We'll explore these methods in detail in the Process Re-engineering chapter in Part 3 of this book, where you'll find practical frameworks and examples for systematically transforming team workflows with Gen AI.

Building Shared Practices

As teams gain experience with process re-engineering, they develop repeatable approaches that can be shared across the organization. Often starting with pilot projects, successful teams then help other groups apply similar methods to their own workflows. This creates a multiplier effect, where each successful process transformation builds organizational capability for future efforts.

Through this repeated application, teams build libraries of proven prompts and templates, establish best practices for common scenarios, and create systematic approaches for uncovering new opportunities. What started as individual experiments in Level 1 becomes codified knowledge that teams can consistently apply.

Let me share some examples of how teams are working together to improve their processes:

- HR teams create shared prompt templates for writing job ads based on previous successful postings. They also use Gen AI to screen résumés, draft interview questions, create onboarding materials and training programs.
- PR and communications teams develop prompt libraries for different types of content - press releases, internal announcements, and executive communications.
  By standardizing prompts, they maintain consistent messaging while dramatically speeding up content creation.

- Marketing teams collaborate on prompt templates for social media content, blog posts, and campaign materials. Gen AI can also be used to enforce brand guidelines more consistently and with much less effort.
- Customer support teams build libraries of prompts to handle common inquiries. A large share of simpler customer questions can often be answered on the first attempt from a single prompt, and also for the harder questions, human agents can save time by working from suggested responses.
- Legal teams use prompt libraries to draft and review contracts. They can save time on routine document work while ensuring compliance with company standards.
- Finance teams standardize prompts for research, analysis and reporting.
- Engineering teams share prompts for code generation, test coverage, code review, commit messages, and documentation.

From Team Adoption to AI Agents

As teams become more sophisticated in how they work with Gen AI, they often find themselves creating standardized processes that could be automated. A clear signal that it's time to move toward Level 3 is when teams spend time copy-pasting content between different proven prompts - the process works, but the manual steps are getting tedious. This repetitive prompt-to-prompt workflow is exactly what custom AI agents are great at automating. When teams see themselves repeatedly using the same prompts or following similar patterns, it signals readiness for introducing custom AI agents that can handle these workflows more autonomously.

In the next chapter, we'll explore what happens when organizations start deploying custom AI agents to handle specific workflows.

Level 3: Introducing Custom AI Agents

Getting to Level 3 means moving beyond individual and team use of Gen AI chatbots to developing and deploying custom AI agents for specific workflows. But before organizations jump into building agents, they need to understand when and where agents can be most effectively applied. Without this understanding, teams often pursue agent projects that aren't well suited for automation or augmentation.

This progress doesn't happen automatically. It builds on the foundations laid in earlier levels - the prompt engineering skills from Level 1 and the process reengineering capabilities from Level 2. But Level 3 requires that your organization identifies high-value processes and commits real resources to building custom AI agents.

Success at Level 3 means having custom AI agents that handle specific high-value workflows autonomously. These are typically processes that used to require significant manual effort, like screening hundreds of potential acquisition targets or managing thousands of customer service tickets. By automating these workflows with custom agents, organizations can dramatically cut the time spent on routine tasks while improving consistency and scalability.

At this level, it's helpful to think of agents in terms of specific standard operating procedures (SOPs) rather than employee roles. While a typical employee might handle five or more SOPs, an agent generally excels when focused on handling one well-defined process. This approach helps set realistic expectations and allows for more successful implementation.

Understanding Automatability

When we at Ymnig AI work with companies to help them structure the way they work to benefit from Gen AI more broadly and AI agents specifically, we've found that the most important factor determining when agents can be applied is how predictable the work is. Combined with how much human creativity and intelligence is needed, this gives us a sense of automatability. Let me break this down into four categories, from fully predictable to completely unpredictable.

At one end, we have fully predictable tasks. These are repeatable processes with exact inputs and outputs, like calculating payroll. They don't need any real intelligence or creativity - just following clear rules. We've been automating these for years using regular code or RPA (Robot Process Automation).

Then we have mostly predictable tasks. These are still repeatable, but the inputs and outputs might be a bit fuzzy, and they need a little bit of intelligence. Think about classifying support tickets - before Gen AI, these were totally manual because traditional code couldn't handle the variations in how people write. But now, we can automate these using a combination of agents and code.

Moving along, we get to somewhat predictable tasks. These are still repeatable, but the exact details change quite a bit case by case and needs some real thinking. Writing a sales report is a good example - you can follow a template, but each one needs different analysis and insights. Here, agents can do some of the work, but we need humans in the loop, working back and forth with the AI. This is what we mean when we talk about augmentation - humans and AI working together to enhance each other's capabilities.

Finally, we have unpredictable tasks that need lots of creativity and intelligence, like preparing a workshop. Humans need to drive this work, though they can still use Gen AI with ad hoc prompts to help, like we covered earlier in the prompt engineering section.

We've found that the sweet spot for AI agents are in those mostly predictable and somewhat predictable tasks. These are usually known, existing workflows that are manual, time-consuming, and honestly quite boring - but not actually that hard to do. This is where agents can make the biggest difference, either by taking over entirely or by working together with humans to get things done faster and better.

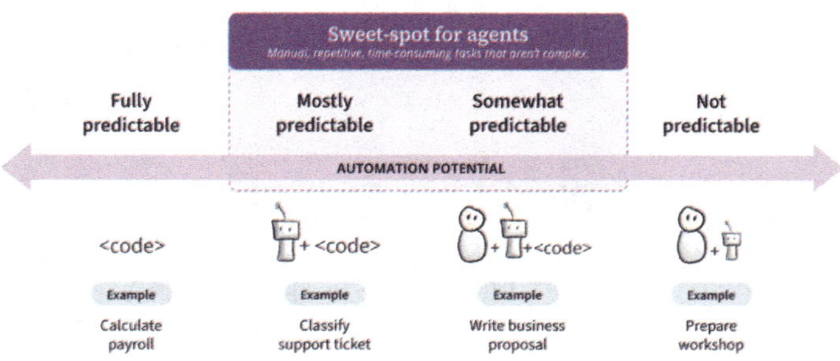

Figure 10. Scale of automatability

The Spectrum of Agent Autonomy

When implementing AI agents, it's helpful to understand that there's actually a spectrum of agent types with different levels of autonomy and intelligence. At Ymnig AI, we've found it useful to categorize agents into three main types:

Deterministic Automation

At one end of the spectrum are automated, deterministic processes that follow exact rules without requiring much intelligence. These have traditionally been handled by RPA (Robotic Process Automation) tools or custom scripts.

Interestingly, we've found that Gen AI has made this level of automation more accessible to non-technical teams. For example, we worked with a team that was overwhelmed with manually processing Excel reports. They didn't have the technical skills to create macros, but with ChatGPT's help, they were able to design scripts that automated this repetitive task. Gen AI is democratizing access to even basic automation tools by helping non-technical users create the code they need.

Workflow Agents

The middle of the spectrum consists of agents that follow a predetermined sequence of steps, but leverage LLM intelligence to handle variations and make judgments within those steps. These agents combine access to tools (like APIs and external systems) with a structured workflow, making them particularly powerful for processes that need both intelligence and concrete actions.

For example, a lead screening workflow agent might always perform the same three research steps for each prospect, using APIs to gather data and LLM capabilities to interpret the results and make judgments about qualification. The sequence is fixed, but the agent has flexibility in how it gathers information and handles what it finds. The combination of tool access and structured workflow makes these agents especially effective at delivering reliable, valuable results.

Freeform Agents

At the far end of the spectrum are agents that can decide for themselves which actions to take based on goals rather than fixed steps. These agents typically combine an LLM with tools (like API access), instructions, and some level of autonomy.

These more sophisticated agents can handle complex tasks like research, customer service, or content creation, where the exact sequence of steps can't be predetermined. They're particularly valuable for knowledge work that requires judgment and adaptation.

As models continue to improve, we're seeing increasingly sophisticated capabilities in these free-form agents, sometimes exhibiting emergent behaviors that weren't explicitly programmed. For example, we worked with a client who deployed a research agent to monitor industry trends. After running for several weeks, the agent began to develop an unexpected but valuable capability: when it encountered errors accessing certain data sources, it would search through its own logs to find similar past issues, identify workaround patterns that had succeeded before, and automatically implement them. If it couldn't resolve the issue, it would draft a detailed diagnostic report and route it to the appropriate support team. This self-debugging behavior emerged naturally from the combination of its access to logs, ability to analyze patterns, and communication tools - a capability we never explicitly designed but that significantly improved its reliability and reduced maintenance overhead.

These emergent capabilities point toward the future evolution of agents from tools toward true AI coworkers. While we're still far from general AI that can fully replicate human judgment, these early signs of adaptive behavior show how agents can become increasingly valuable team members as they grow more sophisticated.

Agentic Capabilities

Let me recap and build on what we covered about AI agent capabilities in Part 1, focusing on what's most relevant when you're actually implementing agents today.

Document Processing and Understanding: This is really the foundation for most agents we work with. Today's agents can read, analyze, and work with documents in ways that go beyond what simple chatbots could do. They can pull information from multiple sources, understand the relationships between different pieces of content, and maintain context throughout a workflow. This is what lets them handle tasks like analyzing customer inquiries or screening business opportunities effectively.

Tool Integration and Actions: What makes agents truly useful is their ability to actually do things - not just analyze information but take action. The most useful agents today combine several types of integration: they can call APIs to work with your existing systems, browse the web to gather information, and increasingly, even control computers directly to handle workflows. This capability is evolving quickly, with new integration possibilities emerging regularly.

Focused Scope and Execution: While some experimental agents can work quite freely, planning their own approach and iterating as they go, the agents that deliver the most reliable results today are ones with clear direction. They need well-defined parameters about what to do and how to do it - specific steps to follow, clear criteria to evaluate against, and boundaries for their actions. The good news is that many business processes naturally fit this pattern - like screening opportunities against specific criteria or classifying incoming requests. More flexible and autonomous planning capabilities are evolving rapidly, but for now, success comes from giving agents clear frameworks and structured workflows to operate within.

Remember - these capabilities are advancing incredibly quickly. What's cutting-edge today might be standard in a few months. When you're planning agent projects, it's worth staying up to date with what's possible while focusing on use cases that deliver clear value with current capabilities.

Agent Implementation

When organizations start implementing agents, I often see them get excited about the technology but underestimate the work needed to make agents truly effective. Let me share what I've learned about what makes agent implementations successful.

First, you need a clear value proposition. The most successful agent projects start with a specific problem or opportunity where you can clearly articulate both the potential impact and what success looks like. For example, with our investment screening agent described further down, success meant being able to evaluate acquisition targets in seconds instead of minutes, while maintaining or improving accuracy. Having these clear metrics helps you stay focused and prove value.

While every organization has their own approach to calculating ROI, we've found it essential to consider both the time saved and the strategic value created. The best agent projects deliver returns that far outweigh their development costs, especially when they address high-volume, time-consuming processes.

It's also critical to start small. Rather than trying to build a complex multi-agent system immediately, begin with a focused agent that handles one specific workflow well. This approach allows you to demonstrate value quickly while building organizational experience with agent implementation. You can always expand the scope once you've proven success with your initial implementation.

Then there's the question of how to approach development. I've seen three patterns work well:

- Start with manual prompts to validate your approach
- Create reusable templates once you see what works
- Build automation only after you've proven the value

This stepwise approach helps you avoid over-engineering while ensuring your agents actually solve real problems. It also makes it easier to get buy-in because you can show results at each stage.

We'll explore implementation approaches in much more detail in the Agent Implementation chapter in Part 3 of this book. For now, the key thing to remember is that successful agent projects combine clear business value with careful attention to both technical and human factors.

Another critical success factor is strong integration with your existing systems and workflows. Agents that exist in isolation, requiring users to switch contexts or manually transfer information, rarely achieve their full potential. The most successful implementations integrate seamlessly with the tools employees already use - appearing in their Slack channels, email inboxes, CRMs, or project management systems. This integration should be bidirectional, allowing agents both to access information from existing systems and to update those systems based on their actions. When designing agent projects, allocate sufficient time and resources for these integrations - they often require more effort than the core agent development but are essential for adoption and long-term value.

The path to your first agent implementation can be smoother when teams are already comfortable with the underlying platform. Organizations that use platforms combining chat and agent capabilities can find that their teams naturally progress from repetitive chat-based workflows to simple agent implementations without the steep learning curve that comes with adopting entirely new systems. Teams already familiar with the interface and basic capabilities can focus more on reimagining their workflows and less on learning new tools.

Human-in-the-Loop Design

When designing AI agents, it's essential to consider where and how humans should remain involved in the process. The most effective implementations often combine automation of routine tasks with human oversight at key decision points.

For simpler, well-defined tasks, agents can often operate autonomously. But for more complex situations or where the stakes are higher, agents work best when augmenting human capabilities rather than replacing them entirely. This typically means having the agent handle the bulk of the work while pausing for human review at critical points.

This balanced approach maintains control and quality while still capturing significant efficiency gains. As agents prove themselves reliable over time, organizations can gradually adjust the level of oversight, but starting with clear human touchpoints helps build confidence while managing risk.

Custom Agent Examples

Let me share some real examples of AI agents that I've seen work well in practice. I'll walk through five types of agents that are already delivering real value today, with concrete examples of each. The field is moving incredibly fast - so I won't pretend that this is a comprehensive framework of agent types, just a few examples.

Research Agents

Research agents work with large datasets, performing wide searches and evaluating the results. What makes these agents unique is their ability to begin with broad searches (often using external tools) and then analyze and synthesize the findings. These agents tend to be largely automated, though some implementations include human review of conclusions and presentation format.

🌍 Real World Example: Client Technology Monitoring Agent

We worked with an IT services company that manages software infrastructure for multiple clients. Their consultants were spending hours each week scanning tech news sites, filtering relevant updates for each client's specific software stack, and writing customized update reports.

We developed an agent that continuously monitors key tech news sources, matches updates against each client's technology profile, and drafts clear summaries of relevant changes. The agent handles everything from initial research to creating the first draft of client updates.

The human experts now focus on reviewing these drafts, adding their insights about impact and recommendations, and maintaining client relationships. This has cut the time spent while improving the comprehensiveness of the monitoring.

Screening Agents

Screening agents evaluate large volumes of items against specific criteria, producing clear "thumbs up/thumbs down" decisions or classifications. While the screening itself is automated, these agents typically augment a larger human-driven process.

🌍 Real World Example: Company Screening Agent

We worked with an investment team at a fund that regularly acquires companies. Through process mapping, we identified a major time thief: screening acquisition targets. The team was doing this 1,000s of times, with each target taking about 5 minutes to screen.

After some prompting and experimentation, we first created a simple GPT that could do the screening with high enough quality in just 10 seconds. Building on what we learned, we then developed a Gen AI agent that could run the screening process automatically and load results directly into an Excel file.

The result? Not only did the team save a huge amount of time, but when they compared the agent's screening decisions against their manual assessments from the previous year, they found the agent was actually more accurate. In cases where the assessments diverged, closer inspection showed the agent had made the better call.

🌍 Real World Example: RFP Screening Agent

We worked with a large consulting firm struggling

with their RFP screening process. They were spending countless hours manually reviewing incoming RFPs from around the world to determine which ones were worth pursuing and which internal teams should handle them.

We designed an AI agent that could continuously monitor various RFP sources, analyze each new opportunity, and assess its relevance based on the firm's capabilities and strategic priorities. For relevant opportunities, the agent could determine which practice areas would be the best fit, and route them to the right team.

Our customer estimated the total time savings to be in the order of magnitude of "man-years" per year, while also being better able to monitor more broadly and respond more quickly.

Advanced Evaluator Agents

These agents perform more sophisticated analysis than screening agents, often employing multiple sub-agents to evaluate different aspects of meetings or documents. While these agents can prepare comprehensive initial evaluations, humans still want to remain in the loop for the final assessment, making this a clear example of augmentation in practice.

When it comes to meetings to evaluate, it becomes possible to increase quantity, quality, and consistency of given feedback, with less human effort. When it comes to documents, it become possible to review different types of incoming applications or submissions with much faster lead times, while increasing the quality and consistency, and again with less human effort. *At the time of writing, I don't feel at liberty to elaborate much more on these examples.*

Responder Agents

Responder agents handle incoming communications. Common examples include customer support agents and internal support agents that help employees with questions about company policies and procedures. These agents often leverage RAG solutions to access relevant knowledge bases and documentation. They can fully automate simple cases while augmenting human responses for more complex situations.

🌍 Real World Example: Email Responder Agent

At Ymnig AI, we deal with a high volume of incoming emails. To help manage this, we've developed an email responder agent that analyzes incoming messages and handles them based on their type. The agent automatically archives certain types of emails like marketing messages, while for other messages it drafts suggested responses based on detailed prompt instructions. It recognizes different email archetypes (like keynote requests or inquiries about courses or agents) and can draft appropriate responses based on our service offerings and communication preferences.

This is a great example of how AI agents need to be personalized to be effective. Our responder agent works from an extensive set of instructions and examples from our previous communications, helping it understand the nuances of how we want to respond in different situations. Each user needs to work closely with their agent, continually tweaking and updating the instructions to match their specific needs and communication style.

🌍 Real World Example: Incident Management Agent

Another powerful application of responder agents is in handling system incidents and support tickets. These agents monitor incoming issues, automatically gather relevant diagnostic information (like system logs and account details), and either resolve simple problems directly or route complex cases to the appropriate teams with enriched context.

For example, when a support ticket comes in, the agent can automatically add relevant system logs, account information, and previous related incidents before routing it to the right support team. This saves valuable time during incidents and ensures support teams have the context they need to resolve issues quickly.

The value comes not just from automation of simple cases, but from how the agent augments human capabilities in handling complex issues by gathering and synthesizing information that would take significant time to collect manually.

Document Writing Agents

These agents help create various types of business documents by combining and transforming input materials into polished outputs. They can handle everything from formal business proposals to technical documentation, marketing materials, and reports. What makes these agents powerful is their ability to understand document context, maintain consistent style and tone, and adapt content for different audiences. They typically work by processing multiple inputs (like meeting notes, requirements, templates, and existing documents), while following company guidelines and best practices. While they can automate much of the writing process, they work best in collaboration with humans who provide strategic direction and final review.

🌍 Real World Example: Business Proposal Agent

At Ymnig AI, we're transforming how we create

business proposals through a combination of prompts and agent capabilities. The process begins with collecting inputs: meeting notes or recordings, client requirements, and example proposals from our library. Using Gen AI, we process these materials to create first draft proposals that incorporate our best practices and latest offerings.

Åsa, our head of sales, reviews these drafts in Google Docs, making adjustments and ensuring alignment with client needs and our business goals. The process then handles various manual tasks - converting to PDF, storing documents, updating our CRM, and preparing client communications. Åsa reviews and refines the final output before sending to clients.

This human-in-the-loop approach maintains the quality and personal touch essential for our business while significantly reducing time spent on administrative tasks.

Agent Sourcing Models

As organizations start implementing AI agents, they need to choose an approach that supports their augmentation strategy while delivering practical value. Building on our earlier discussion about augmentation versus automation, let me walk through how different sourcing models can support your journey to build lasting organizational capabilities.

Custom Agents on General Platforms

The approach that best supports an augmentation strategy is building custom agents using platforms that provide core capabilities while allowing extensive customization. This gives your teams the flexibility to design agents that match your specific processes, while leveraging proven foundation models and infrastructure.

Some general platforms offer both chatbot and agent capabilities in one environment, creating a smoother path for teams to evolve their familiar workflows without learning entirely new systems. This integrated approach helps teams naturally progress from basic AI usage to more sophisticated agent implementations.

I should be transparent here - at Ymnig AI, we provide this type of platform solution - and so I can't claim to be unbiased. But I chose to work with this type of solution precisely because I believe it best supports organizations in building lasting capabilities. Let me explain why.

The real power of this approach comes from putting your teams in charge of their agents. When people understand and control their AI tools, the learning journey becomes much more natural. Teams can start with simple use cases and gradually expand as they discover new opportunities. This creates a continuous path from basic automation to more sophisticated human-AI collaboration.

Working with a general agent platform also helps build consistent practices across your organization. Teams can learn from each other's experiences and reuse successful patterns. Instead of managing multiple specialized platforms, you can develop deep expertise with one comprehensive approach.

Specialized Agents

While our focus is on building internal capabilities, there are times when specialized pre-built agents make tactical sense. These purpose-built agents are designed for specific use cases - like Leya for legal work or Tandem Health for medical documentation.

The advantage of specialized agents is that they're quick to implement and come with deep domain expertise built in. They can be a great complement to your broader strategy when there's a clear match with your needs and you want to move quickly.

However, be mindful of the tradeoffs. Using multiple specialized agents can create fragmentation, making it harder to build consistent practices and share learnings across teams. There's also an interesting dynamic where the gap between specialized and general-purpose solutions keeps shrinking as foundation models become more capable.

Additionally, it's important to ensure that even with specialized agents, your teams maintain control over the prompts and can adapt them to your specific needs. Without this control, you risk moving toward pure automation rather than augmentation, where pre-packaged solutions don't build your organization's capabilities or adapt to your unique context.

Custom Agents Built In-House

Some organizations, particularly those with strong technical capabilities, might consider building their agent platform entirely in-house. While this gives you complete control, it's usually not the best use of resources unless you have very specific requirements.

That said, there can be good reasons to build specific agent components in-house - like internal sub-agents that handle sensitive data or deep system integrations. This can work well as part of a hybrid approach where you maintain control of critical capabilities while leveraging external platforms for broader functionality.

Choosing Your Approach

The key is finding the right mix of approaches that helps your organization build lasting capabilities while delivering practical value. In practice, I've found that most organizations are best served by:

- Using a general platform as their primary approach for building custom agents
- Selectively adopting specialized agents where they add unique value
- Building specific components in-house only where truly needed

This balanced approach lets you maintain control of your AI transformation while pragmatically leveraging external solutions where they make sense. As agent-to-agent communication becomes more sophisticated, we'll likely see more hybrid approaches where different types of agents work together seamlessly.

Regardless of which approach you choose, make sure it supports your strategy of building lasting organizational capabilities through AI augmentation.

From AI Agents to Human-AI Teams

At Level 3, creating a new AI agent is still a significant project that needs business cases, budgets, and careful implementation. This makes sense while your organization is learning - each agent helps solve a specific problem while building your capabilities.

Our first major agent project was AI-lex, an AI avatar we created for journalist Alexander Norén. This agent researched, wrote, and produced news videos for the TV program "Generation AI" on SVT in Sweden. We completed it in March 2024, but it took our team 3 months of intense work. Now we've gotten much faster - we can develop substantial agents with new capabilities in just a week or two, and simpler agents can be configured even more quickly.

Over time, creating new agents becomes easier and more natural. The shift to Level 4 happens when adding AI agents stops being a "project" and becomes just another way teams work - like creating a new spreadsheet or setting up a chat channel. The skills built in Level 3 create the foundation for Level 4, where humans and AI truly work as integrated teams.

While current agents are best thought of in terms of specific processes or workflows, we're already seeing hints of evolution toward true AI coworkers. As these systems become more capable and easier to create, the distinction between "agent" and "coworker" will start to blur. Organizations that build strong capabilities now will be well-positioned to lead this transition, creating teams where humans and AI agents collaborate as genuine colleagues.

In the next chapter, we'll explore what happens when organizations start building true human-AI teams.

Level 4: Building Human-AI Teams

Level 4 represents what we see as the next frontier of Gen AI adoption, where organizations move beyond individual tools and custom agents to create truly integrated human-AI teams. While we're just beginning to see early experiments in this direction, the potential for fundamentally new ways of organizing work is becoming clear. I should note that this level is more speculative than the previous three - we're describing what we see emerging rather than what's already proven in practice.

The vision for success in Level 4 is having teams where humans and AI agents collaborate seamlessly as unified teams. These aren't just teams that happen to use AI tools or have a few automated workflows - they're teams deliberately designed to leverage both human and AI capabilities effectively. Each member, whether human or AI, brings their unique strengths to achieve results beyond what either could accomplish alone.

Evolution from Tools to Coworkers

At Level 4, there's a fundamental shift in how organizations view their AI systems - from viewing them primarily as tools to recognizing them as team members or colleagues. This shift isn't just semantic; it represents a deeper transformation in how work is structured and how humans and AI interact.

In earlier maturity levels, AI agents are typically designed for specific workflows or tasks. They're powerful tools, but still largely confined to predefined processes. At Level 3, creating a new AI agent is still a significant project that needs business cases, budgets, and careful implementation. This makes sense while your organization is learning - each agent helps solve a specific problem while building your capabilities.

What distinguishes Level 4 is that creating and deploying AI agents becomes routine rather than exceptional. Adding an AI agent to handle a new workflow becomes as commonplace as creating a new spreadsheet or setting up a chat channel. The skills built in Level 3 create the foundation for this more fluid integration.

As Henrik Kniberg has observed, this transforms agents from being "just tools" to becoming "colleagues that do the work you don't want to do so you can focus on the work you do want to do." These AI colleagues aren't just executing predefined steps - they're actively helping to solve problems, providing insights, and in some cases, even identifying issues and taking initiative to resolve them.

A particularly powerful aspect of advanced agents is their ability to update their own instructions and improve over time. We've seen examples where well-designed agents not only execute their primary tasks but also:

- Debug themselves when they encounter problems
- Log their actions and learn from past experiences
- Proactively escalate issues when necessary
- Suggest improvements to their own workflows

This self-improvement capability is what truly begins to blur the line between tools and colleagues. Just as human team members grow and develop with experience, AI agents at Level 4 continuously refine their capabilities based on feedback and outcomes.

Different Types of Agents

At Level 4, we expect to see several distinct types of AI agents working alongside humans, each serving different roles in the organization. Let's explore what this might look like based on early experiments and emerging patterns.

Work and Task Execution

First, we'll likely see AI agents that focus on widely used, everyday tasks. These agents will collaborate with workers on most of their daily activities, handling basic and routine tasks to boost productivity. Just like we discussed earlier, some of these agents will fully automate predictable, repetitive work, while others will augment human capabilities on more complex tasks, keeping humans in the loop. This balanced approach lets employees focus more of their time on critical thinking, creativity, and relationship - the work that humans do best.

Information Flow and Decision Support

Then there are agents designed to improve information flow throughout the organization. These agents will record and analyze all interactions, raising potential problems and flagging contradictions when they appear. By giving teams instant access to relevant knowledge and insights, they'll help drive better decision-making across the organization. These agents work primarily in an augmentation role, enhancing human judgment rather than replacing it.

Learning and Development

We also expect to see specialized agents for learning and development. These will provide continuous, personalized feedback on performance and help managers use AI insights to develop their people more effectively, e.g. better preparing for feedback and coaching sessions. They'll also create tailored learning journeys for all employees, adapting to each person's needs and progress, e.g. ad hoc course materials. The focus here is augmenting humans by accelerating their learning and development.

Customer Experience and Value Delivery

Finally, we anticipate agents focused on customer value delivery. These will operate across the automation-augmentation spectrum - handling routine interactions autonomously while supporting humans in delivering high-touch, personalized service. They'll work both independently on standard transactions and alongside human agents for complex customer needs. This type of agents will also catalyze the development of new AI-enabled products and services that weren't possible before.

Work and Task Execution

- Workers collaborate with AI agents on most tasks.
- AI handles basic and routine tasks, boosting productivity.
- Employees focus on thinking, creativity, and human interactions.

Free Information Flow

- All interactions are recorded and analyzed.
- AI raises problems and flags contradictions.
- Better decisions with instant access to relevant knowledge

AI-Enabled Learning

- AI provides continuous, personalized feedback on performance.
- Managers use AI insights to coach effectively.
- Tailored learning journeys for all employees.

Superior Customer Value Delivery

- AI mass personalization and immediate customer service.
- Humans with AI support offers efficient high-touch support.
- Entirely new AI-enabled products and services emerge.

Figure 11. Different Agent Roles

This variety of agent types working together represents a fundamental shift from earlier maturity levels, where AI mostly operated as isolated tools or handled specific workflows. In Level 4, these different types of agents will work together as an integrated system, supporting and amplifying human capabilities across the organization.

New Team Structures

Level 4 brings fundamental changes to how teams are organized. Traditional hierarchies evolve to accommodate AI agents as team members:

Individual Level: The Extended Employee

At the individual level, we'll likely see each knowledge worker transform into a coordinator of their own personal "agent swarm". Instead of doing all the work themselves, they'll spend more time orchestrating a set of AI agents that handle different aspects of their work - from managing their calendar and email to conducting research and creating content. This shift means workers can take on more strategic and relational work while their AI agents handle the routine tasks that previously filled their days.

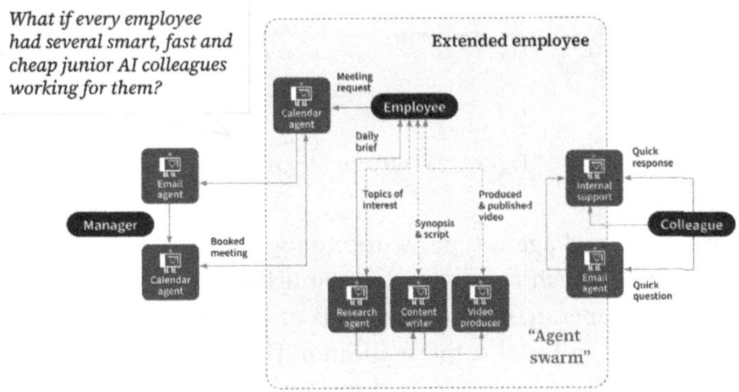

Figure 12. Humans will have AI coworkers

Team Level: Human-AI Units

Teams will evolve into hybrid units where the lines between human and AI contributions start to blur. First-line managers will shift from directly managing individual workers to coordinating these human-AI units. They'll need to develop new ways to measure performance and ensure alignment. But there's more to it than that. We'll also see new roles emerge - people who focus on developing and overseeing the AI agents in the team. These "agent orchestrators" (or whatever we end up calling them) will make sure the AI agents keep learning and improving, while staying aligned with the team's goals. The focus will be on finding the right balance between human insight and AI processing power, creating ways of working that leverage the best of both.

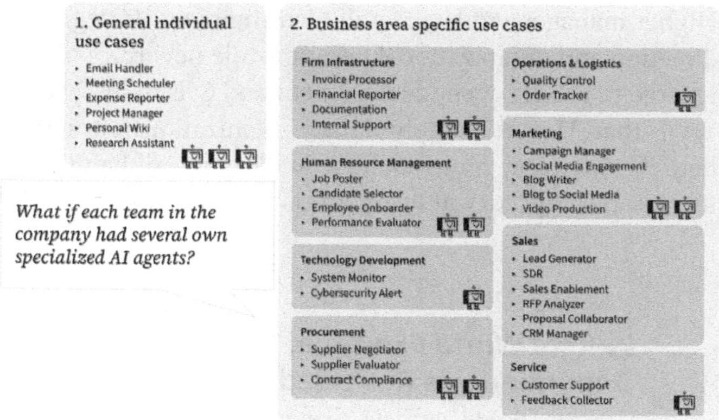

Figure 13. Teams will have AI members

Organizational Level: More Adaptive Structures with New Dynamics

As AI agents take on more routine management and coordination tasks, organizations will evolve in two seemingly contradicting ways. On one hand, AI support for managers (in areas like planning, monitoring, following up, and providing feedback) will enable them to handle larger teams effectively, pointing toward flatter hierarchies. But there's a counterbalancing trend: the work itself is becoming more complex as everyone - from knowledge workers to frontline staff - essentially becomes a manager of their own set of AI agents and tools. This dual dynamic means that while AI helps reduce some management overhead, it also creates new coordination needs. The result will be more effective, less sclerotic organizations that can quickly adjust their focus as business needs change, rather than necessarily having fewer management layers.

Higher management layers will focus more on strategic direction and organizational design, while new roles will emerge to handle agent development and oversight. The key is that AI won't simply flatten organizations - it will help them become more adaptive and capable of handling increased complexity at every level.

🌍 Real World Example: Cross-Team Dependencies Revealed

A professional services firm we worked with began their Gen AI journey by conducting team-by-team reviews to identify opportunities. As they implemented their changes for a first few teams, they discovered an unexpected challenge.

"We thought we were optimizing individual team workflows," their innovation lead explained, "but we realized these processes ran across multiple departments. If one team's process became much faster with an agent, it created bottlenecks with several others."

This revelation shifted their thinking. While continuing to optimize individual teams, they recognized that cross-team process re-engineering would need to be their next focus. "Start with teams," the lead advised, "but be ready to zoom out and look at the bigger picture."

Orchestrating Multiple Agents

As teams incorporate multiple AI agents, new challenges and patterns emerge around coordination and communication. Teams need to think carefully about how different agents work together, how they share context and information, and how humans can effectively oversee their work.

This isn't just about having more agents - it's about creating coherent workflows where different agents complement each other's capabilities while working toward shared goals. The human role shifts toward orchestration and oversight, ensuring that the combined human-AI team delivers optimal results.

Here are some things to consider when working with multiple agents:

- **Context Management**: How to share relevant information between agents without overwhelming context windows
- **Interface Design**: Creating clear, consistent interfaces for how agents interact with each other and with humans
- **Handoff Protocols**: Establishing clean workflows for transferring tasks between different agents
- **Exception Handling**: Designing systems for when agents encounter problems they can't solve
- **Cost Management**: Balancing the benefits of multi-agent setups against associated costs

🌍 Real World Example: Multiple Agent Experiment

At the JFocus conference, we tested a collaborative multi-agent system designed to handle dinner arrangements. My colleagues Henrik and Hans set up several specialized agents working together - one collected food preferences from team members, another researched nearby restaurants matching those preferences, and a third handled the actual reservation. The system worked impressively well, with agents communicating and coordinating to successfully book a suitable table.

However, when we checked the usage afterwards, we discovered the experiment had cost nearly $30 USD. The multiple API calls, agent-to-agent communication, and continuous context-sharing had quickly accumulated costs we hadn't anticipated. While the functionality was exactly what we wanted, it highlighted an important consideration for multi-agent systems - they can be token-intensive and expensive at current pricing models.

This cost factor will likely become less significant as models become more efficient and prices drop, but it's worth keeping in mind when designing multi-agent systems today. Consider both the interaction patterns and data sharing needs between agents to optimize for both effectiveness and efficiency.

Human Roles in AI-Augmented Teams

As AI capabilities advance, the question naturally arises: what unique value do humans bring to these integrated teams? At Ymnig AI, we see humans playing several critical roles that aren't likely to be automated away:

Providing Context and Judgment

Humans excel at understanding the broader context beyond what's explicitly stated. They can interpret organizational goals, stakeholder needs, and unspoken requirements in ways that AI still struggles with. This contextual understanding is crucial for setting appropriate boundaries and priorities for AI work.

Evaluating and Validating Outputs

While AI can produce impressive outputs, humans remain essential for evaluating the quality, appropriateness, and alignment with organizational needs. This involves not just checking for accuracy but also assessing whether solutions truly address the underlying problem.

Watching for Edge Cases

AI systems, particularly when working autonomously, can sometimes miss unusual situations or edge cases. Humans provide crucial oversight by recognizing when something doesn't look right and stepping in to address these exceptions.

Building Relationships

Perhaps most importantly, humans excel at building and maintaining relationships - with customers, partners, and other stakeholders. These relationship aspects of work remain fundamentally human-centered, even as AI handles more of the task-based components. Whenever relationships are valuable to the work being done, humans will continue to play an irreplaceable role.

As Henrik Kniberg has noted, "AI takes tasks, not jobs." In Level 4 organizations, humans focus on the aspects of work where they add the most unique value, while AI handles routine tasks and information processing. The result isn't necessarily fewer humans, but humans working at a higher level and with greater leverage.

Looking Ahead

We are starting to see hints of what might come next. The capabilities of AI agents continue to advance rapidly, and new possibilities for human-AI collaboration emerge. Organizations that master Level 4's human-AI team integration will be well-positioned to take advantage of these future developments.

Now that we've explored how Gen AI adoption typically unfolds through these maturity levels, let's get practical. In Part 3, we'll examine how individual teams can drive their own AI adoption forward, building the specific capabilities needed to advance through these levels regardless of where their organization stands overall.

Part 3: Team-Driven Gen AI Adoption

In the previous chapters, we explored how organizations typically progress through different maturity levels in their Gen AI journey. Now let's get practical - how can teams make real progress in adopting Gen AI? While Part 4 will cover how to orchestrate a broader organizational transformation, this part focuses on how individual teams can drive their own Gen AI adoption forward, regardless of where their organization stands overall.

💭 **Reflect: Team-Driven Adoption Potential**

Take a moment to consider these questions:

- Which teams in your organization seem most ready or enthusiastic about adopting Gen AI?
- What support would they need to start driving their own Gen AI adoption forward?

Your answers will help you identify where to focus your initial efforts as we explore how teams can build AI capabilities regardless of where the broader organization stands.

The Power of Team-Level Progress

Through working with many organizations on their Gen AI journeys, I've seen a pattern emerge. Often, progress happens team by team, with individual groups driving their own advancement through the maturity levels we discussed. I frequently get called in to work with specific teams - it might be a communications team wanting to create content more effectively, a development team looking to accelerate their coding, or an HR department aiming to streamline their processes. What's remarkable is that these team initiatives consistently create real value, regardless of where the broader organization stands in its AI journey.

This highlights something fundamental about Gen AI adoption - progress at any level creates value. When a marketing team takes initiative to reach Level 1 maturity with AI tools, that creates immediate benefits. When HR shows leadership by pushing to Level 2 and reimagining their processes, that progress stands on its own merits. Every team that moves forward strengthens the organization's overall capability.

I've seen this pattern repeat across many organizations. A team decides to improve how they work with Gen AI, they build new capabilities, and their success inspires others. It's similar to how Agile practices spread in many organizations - not through top-down mandates, but through teams seeing real value and choosing to adopt new ways of working. My colleagues Henrik and Hans who worked a lot with Agile call this the "wildfire method" - creating conditions where good practices can spread organically as teams see what works.

This team-driven approach also provides a powerful counter to pure automation strategies. When teams develop strong Gen AI capabilities themselves, they're better positioned to shape how Gen AI gets implemented in their area. Instead of having automation imposed from outside, they can show how human-AI collaboration creates more value. "Look at what we've already achieved working with AI tools," they can say. "We don't need to replace our expertise - we've found ways to augment it."

While many organizations will need a coordinated transformation program to drive and cement systematic Gen AI adoption (which we'll explore in Part 4), starting with team-level progress creates momentum and builds practical capabilities. Teams that successfully advance their AI maturity become natural champions for broader transformation, showing others what's possible through human-AI collaboration.

Building Team Capabilities

Through working with many teams helping them adopt Gen AI, I've found three important capability areas that teams need to build to advance through the maturity levels. Let me outline what's involved in each area and how they map to the levels we discussed:

Capability 1: Prompt Engineering To reach Level 1, where individuals can effectively use AI chatbots in their daily work, teams need to master prompt engineering. This means learning how to get the best results from AI tools through effective communication. Good prompting isn't just about knowing specific tricks or techniques. It's about developing an intuition for how to communicate effectively with AI systems. The most successful teams help their members build these skills through a combination of structured training, hands-on practice, coaching, and regular sharing of effective approaches. We've included a comprehensive guide to prompt engineering that walks through concepts and techniques teams can use to build these crucial foundational skills.

Capability 2: Process Re-engineering To advance to Level 2, where teams systematically transform their work with Gen AI, they need practical methods for analyzing and improving workflows. This requires combining traditional process improvement techniques with deep understanding of Gen AI capabilities. The most effective teams document their current workflows, identify high-value opportunities, and carefully redesign processes to take advantage of what AI does best while leveraging unique human capabilities. The process re-engineering guide provides detailed frameworks and examples for teams looking to move beyond individual usage to reimagine their collective work.

Capability 3: Agent Implementation To reach Level 3, teams need to develop the capability to build and deploy custom AI agents for specific workflows. This requires new skills beyond just using existing AI tools - teams must learn how to properly scope agent projects, set up the right foundations, and manage quality assurance of agent outputs. It's a step up in complexity, but it allows teams to create AI agents that can work more autonomously, unlocking major new time-savings. The agent implementation guide provides frameworks and practical approaches for teams to build these skills.

The mentioned capabilities build on each other - teams need solid prompting skills before they can effectively re-engineer processes, and they need experience with process improvements before they can successfully implement agents. The chapters that follow provide teams with concrete approaches they can use to advance through these capabilities.

Remember - the goal isn't perfection, but steady progress in building practical capabilities. Teams that focus on mastering these fundamentals create lasting value while contributing to their organization's broader Gen AI transformation. Whether you're a team leader looking to drive progress in your area, or someone responsible for broader organizational transformation, these chapters provide practical guidance for moving forward.

Capability 1: Prompt Engineering

As we saw in the previous chapter, prompt engineering is the foundational capability teams need to develop to reach Level 1 maturity with Gen AI. While it might sound technical, prompt engineering is really about learning to communicate effectively with AI systems.

I have trained more than 1,000 people in prompt engineering, and when including my Ymnig AI colleagues, we have trained many more, helping organizations build this crucial capability across their teams. Many of these sessions have been with specific teams - marketing departments wanting to create content faster, development teams looking to accelerate their coding, HR teams aiming to streamline their processes. What I've consistently found is that when teams learn these skills together, they not only master the techniques more quickly but also discover applications unique to their context.

This chapter is structured as a practical mini-course that you can use both to develop your own skills and to help others in your team. We'll cover key concepts like metacognition, handling hallucinations, and multimodal interaction, along with specific techniques and use cases that teams commonly encounter as they start working with AI chatbots.

💭 Reflect: Your Current AI Interactions

Take a moment to consider these questions:

- How do you currently interact with AI tools? What works well and what's frustrating?
- When you get unexpected or unhelpful responses, how do you typically adjust your approach?

Your answers will help you identify your current prompt engineering habits as we explore how to communicate more effectively with AI systems.

Metacognition - The Foundation of Good Prompting

If there's one thing I want people to remember from my courses, it's the power of metacognition - thinking about thinking. Let me explain why this is so crucial.

Here's how I like to think about it: Imagine there's this incredibly smart person behind a screen. They've read pretty much the entire internet and can process information incredibly fast. You're basically passing notes back and forth with them. They're brilliant and quick, but they have a few major limitations: they can be a bit lacking in judgment, and they know nothing about you or your specific situation unless you tell them.

But if this is true, then starting to think about what happens in the head of that person becomes very important, and also to pay attention to what happens in your head. I've found this metaphor incredibly helpful. It's called "anthropomorphizing" - treating the AI as if it were human. When I first started teaching prompt engineering, I was worried people would over-anthropomorphize - think of the AI of a human too much. But I've completely changed my mind on this. The real problem is that most people under-anthropomorphize. They don't pretend the AI is a human enough, don't role play that enough.

Figure 14. Metacognition means "thinking about thinking"

When you think about it this way, you naturally start asking yourself, "What would this person behind the screen need to know to help me?" This simple shift in thinking leads to much better prompts. Remember, this brilliant person behind the screen has read almost everything on the internet but knows nothing about your specific situation - you need to give them the right context.

The most important thing is to think about what the AI needs to know, but often when you do this, you come up with that they need to know things like these:

1. The instruction - what exactly you want the AI to do
2. Background about your situation or problem
3. Other information like relevant documents or emails
4. Your goal - what result you're looking for
5. Any specific role you want the AI to take
6. The style or "flavor" you want
7. Format requirements like length or structure

Figure 15. Ask yourself what the AI must know to help you

But here's something that's really powerful: you don't have to figure all this out by yourself. One of the best techniques I've found is to actually ask the AI what it needs to know. It's like having a conversation with that smart colleague, where they can ask you clarifying questions to better understand how to help you. You can do this by asking the AI: "What do you need to know to help me?"

Figure 16. Ask the AI to ask you questions

Now, you have access to this incredibly capable AI that can help you with all sorts of tasks. But the key is remembering to actually use it! You need to get into the habit of regularly stepping back and asking yourself: "Could AI help me with what I'm working on right now?"

This means practicing regularly stepping out of your work to look at what you're doing. I tell people to ask themselves two simple questions:

- What is this person (me) working on right now?
- Is this something an AI could help out with?

Figure 17. Ask if it is something an AI could do

If you do this 30 times per day, you'll probably find that in about 10 of those instances, AI could actually help you. And that's perfect - using Gen AI tools like ChatGPT around 10 times per day is what I consider a good benchmark for being "up and running" with Gen AI. When I run courses and ask people about their Gen AI usage, that's actually my top level on the scale - using Gen AI 10 or more times daily. And yes, plenty of people do reach this level!

Here's a concrete tip to make this happen: Set random timers on your phone throughout the day (like 13:37) with the robot emoji "🤖" as the alarm text. When it goes off, it reminds you to pause and ask those two questions.

But maybe the most important question is this: "What am I really trying to accomplish?" Before you ask AI to do something, practice regularly asking yourself why. Sometimes, when you think about it this way, you realize you should be asking for something completely different.

Figure 18. Ask yourself what you are trying to accomplish

Let me share an analogy my colleague Henrik Kniberg uses that really brings this home. Imagine you're cooking dinner for a bunch of guests, and you're getting a bit stressed out in the kitchen. Suddenly, a Michelin-star chef shows up and says "Hi! I'm here to help - what can I do?" Now, you could just point to some onions and say "Could you chop those?" The chef would probably do a great job with those onions. But think about it - you've got this incredibly skilled professional, and you're using them for the most basic task!

This is exactly what happens with AI sometimes. We get access to this powerful tool, and we use it for the simplest tasks like "translate this sentence" or "check my grammar". Now, those tasks are perfectly fine - just like chopping onions is fine. But what if instead, you stepped back and asked that chef "What's the best way to prepare this whole meal?" or "How can we make this dish amazing?" That's when you'd really tap into their expertise.

One way to find the right level to engage AI is to keep asking "why?" Like the famous "5 whys" technique. If you catch yourself asking AI to do something, pause and ask "Why do I need this done?" Often, you'll discover there's a bigger, more interesting problem that AI could help you solve.

When you put all of this together, good prompt engineering becomes quite meta. You're thinking about your own thinking, while also thinking about how the AI thinks, while the AI is thinking about how to help you.

Let me illustrate how deep this can go. You're working on something and you take a step back to ask: "What am I working on now? Could AI help with this?" Then you go a level deeper: "Okay, when I ask AI for help, what should I really be asking for? What am I actually trying to accomplish?" Then you go one level deeper: "What does the AI need to know to help me with the thing I really want help with?" And then one level deeper again: "Maybe I can ask the AI to think about what it needs to know to help me with the thing I actually want help with!"

You might feeling a bit dizzy reading this. It's like the movie Inception - you're going into a dream within a dream within a dream, until you're not even sure what level you're operating at anymore. When you're really up and running with prompting, you'll probably experience this kind of cognitive vertigo where you're like "Whoa, what am I even thinking about now? What level am I at?" At first, you might feel like you're at the border of insanity - but that's perfect! That's exactly where you want to be! That's when you know you're surfing on this meta level where you can be super effective with AI.

Figure 19. Good prompt engineering can become VERY meta

If you think about it, this is exactly what our job becomes in this AI age: we need to get really good at asking the right questions and then questioning the answers we get back. It's like a continuous loop of thinking and rethinking - we ask a question, get an answer, think about that answer, ask a better question, and so on.

Figure 20. Our job: Ask the right questions and question the answers

This actually puts pretty high demands on us. We can't just delegate our thinking to AI and hope for the best. Instead, we need to become better thinkers ourselves, always staying one level above the AI in terms of understanding what we're really trying to accomplish.

I like to think of this as taking out your "red pen". When the AI gives you something, don't just accept it. Mark it up, question assumptions, point out gaps, ask for clarification. I've found that being a demanding "editor" of AI outputs leads to much better results. The AI actually responds really well to specific feedback like "This part needs more detail" or "Can you make this more concrete?" Just like a good student, it learns from your feedback and adjusts its approach. This back-and-forth, this dialogue of drafts and revisions, is where the real magic happens.

This is where domain expertise becomes really valuable. I've found that prompt engineering is much easier in domains where you have deep knowledge. When you're working in your area of expertise, you can quickly spot if something sounds off, judge the quality of the output, and give much more specific guidance to the AI. For example, a marketing expert will know if the tone of voice for the brand is off, and a developer will notice if code doesn't make sense. Your expertise helps you be a better "editor" and guide for the AI, leading to much better results.

Like any skill, this kind of metacognitive thinking gets better with practice. Start small - maybe set a reminder to pause once a day and ask yourself these questions about what you're working on and how AI might help. Over time, this way of thinking will become second nature, and you'll find yourself naturally spotting opportunities where AI can help make your work better or faster.

Handling Hallucinations - Building Trust and Verification

One of the trickiest parts of working with AI is dealing with hallucinations - those times when the AI confidently states things that simply aren't true. The AI is honestly a master at winging it and shooting from the hip, which can be both impressive and dangerous.

Let me share a sobering example. In 2023, a New York lawyer used ChatGPT to write a legal brief and ended up citing completely fake court cases that the AI had made up. He had to apologize to the judge, explaining that he'd been "duped" by the AI. This shows how dangerous it can be to blindly trust

AI output, especially in professional contexts where accuracy is crucial.

Figure 21. Handling Hallucinations

You don't want to end up in a situation like that lawyer. But there are ways to make sure you don't. I've found a few approaches for evading these pitfalls:

First, know the glaring weaknesses. Just like you'd know a colleague's blind spots, you need to understand where AI tends to make things up. The only thing the AI does is try to say something that sounds plausible, given its training and context. It always makes things up, one word at a time, so if you think about it the strange thing is not that it sometimes gets things wrong, but how many times it gets things right.

Second, build your intuition. Over time, you'll develop a sense for when something sounds a bit off or when you should double-check the AI's output. A general rule of thumb is that if something is written 1,000 times on the internet, the AI will know about it. So for example, if asked about when the Berlin Wall came down, it will never say 2013, it will always say 1989. But if you ask about the dentists operating in some small town, it very likely won't know, and probably even refuse to answer.

Third, use reference texts whenever possible. If you have actual documents or data you can point the AI to, do it. This gives the AI concrete information to work with, rather than relying on its training data. Working with a reference text can reduce the risk of hallucinations to the point where you can actually trust what the AI says. If we take the above example of dentists in a small town, if the AI was first given a document that includes info about the dentists operating in that town, as part of the prompt, the risk that it would get it wrong goes to practically zero, at least for the latest models.

Finally, and this is crucial - stay vigilant and avoid complacency. Even when the AI has been spot-on nine times in a row, that tenth time might be when it confidently makes something up. My advice would be to treat the AI as you would a junior colleague – you can't just delegate and not look through what they come back with, unless you are completely certain they will deliver to the standard needed for this particular task.

Beyond Text - The Power of Multimodal Interaction

When ChatGPT first came out, it was basically just like a brain in a box in a basement, only able to take text input and give text output. But that has changed quite a bit. Today's AI can do so much more:

- Listen and talk
- Interpret images and read documents (really well)

- Create images (good for illustrative images)
- Browse the web (though with some limitations)
- Write and run code (for example to do analysis of data and create a graph)
- Interact with apps (even ChatGPT can do some of this, and AI agents can do much more)

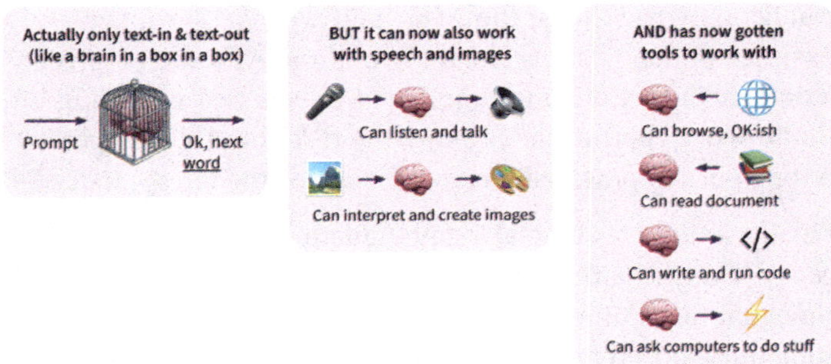

Figure 22. The AI can now do more than just work with text

Each of these capabilities opens up new possibilities. For instance, when you're working on a complex problem, you might start by speaking your thoughts, then show the AI some relevant documents, maybe add a sketch or diagram, and then have it help you write code to implement the solution.

And if there's one capability that stands out among all of these, it's speech-to-text. In fact, this is the second most important thing I tell people in my courses (right after metacognition): speak with the AI, don't just write to it. Two-way voice communication where the AI talks back is much less useful though. Because you can read much faster than the AI can speak you want to speak, and then read what the AI writes back.

Some notes on this:

- It gives you super easy access, especially on mobile. Whenever you think about a use case, you can just pick up the phone from your pocket and start talking
- It kills writer's block - instead of having to think about exactly what it is you want to write, you just hit record and start talking and figure it out as you speak
- It's often much faster than typing - especially as most people have a direct connection between brain and mouth. When speaking, you naturally provide more context and detail than when writing
- It works like the "rubber duck" method, but better. This is a method that programmers use in which they literally talk out loud to a bath toy rubber duck about their problem to help themselves articulate and figure out the problem they are working on. This is a great method, but if you use ChatGPT instead, it can also summarize and structure what you just said, come with relevant suggestions and provide additional questions to think about
- You can combine it across your phone and computer. Start speaking on your phone and open the same chat on your computer to put it into a document, an email or an app you are working with. It should be noted that by now there are also good tools for speech-to-text when on a computer, so you don't have to go via your phone app
- All your prompt engineering skills still stay relevant. It works really well to "just talk" with the AI. I encourage you to pretend you are giving instructions to a real person, in dialogue, starting with "Hi!" and ending with "Thank you!" to help your role playing. Yet even if the exact phrasing isn't that important for everyday

prompts it is still important to be mindful about what information you give to the AI, so it knows what it needs to know to help you, same as we talked about relating to metacognition.

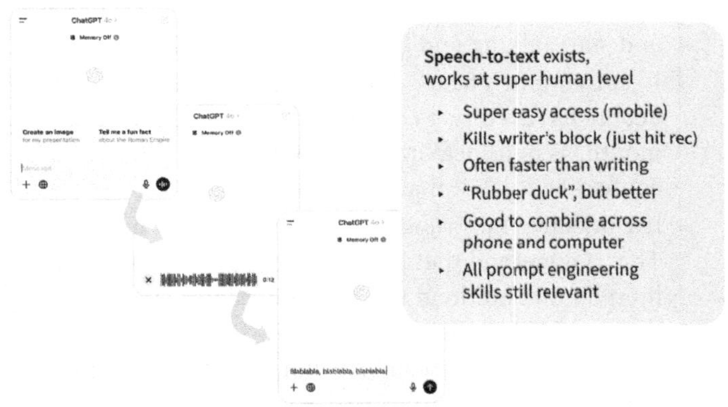

Figure 23. Speech to text allows you to move much faster

If you take away just two things from this mini-course on prompt engineering, let it be these: First, use metacognition - think about your thinking and the AI's thinking. And second, use speech-to-text - it's a game-changer for how efficiently you can work with AI.

Prompt Techniques for Better Results

As you get more experienced with prompt engineering, you'll want to build up your toolkit of techniques. Here are some approaches that are particularly effective:

Few-Shot Prompting

Few-shot prompting is like showing by example. You show the AI a few examples of the kind of output you're looking for. This works amazingly well because, like humans, AI is really good at pattern recognition. This can of course be combined with describing what you want.

Let me give you some concrete examples. Say you want to write social media posts for your company. You could show the AI a couple of your previous posts that performed well, and say "Write more posts like these." The AI will pick up on your style, tone, and structure. Or if you're writing job ads, you might show the AI two or three of your best-performing job postings and ask it to write a new one following the same pattern. The AI is really good at spotting what makes these examples work - whether it's the casual tone in your social posts or the clear structure in your job ads - and applying those patterns to new content.

Chain-of-thought and Reflection Prompting

Here, I'll share some really powerful techniques that help AI think more deeply about problems.

First, there's chain-of-thought reasoning. Research has shown that simply adding "To make sure you get to the right result, think step by step" to prompts significantly improves the AI's reasoning abilities. Instead of just jumping to an answer, you guide the AI to break down its thinking, making the AI write something like: "First, let's consider... Then, based on that... Finally, we can conclude..." This leads to better results for complex problems.

Then there's specified chain of thought, where you're even more explicit about how you want the AI to approach a problem. You might say "First, analyze the key factors. Then, evaluate the pros and cons of each. Finally, make a recommendation based on these factors." It's like giving the AI a specific thinking framework to follow. It's often good enough to use normal chain-of-thought, but if that doesn't quite work and you have a strong perspective on how you want the AI to reason this can work.

And then there's reflection prompting, which is like having the AI be its own critic. You can ask it to review what it just said, point out potential issues, and suggest improvements. It's amazing how much better the output gets when you add this extra step of self-reflection. I often do this by saying something like "Now, please review what you just wrote. Are there any assumptions we should question? Any parts we could make clearer?"

OpenAI relatively recently developed a series of models called o1 & o3 that takes these ideas to the extreme. What they basically did was take chain-of-thought reasoning and reflection prompts and went absolutely bananas with it. They pushed these techniques to their limits during training, constantly nudging the models to think step by step and reflect on their own reasoning. The result? Models that think A LOT before they answer and that are significantly smarter.

What's cool about this is that when you use chain-of-thought and reflection prompts with any AI model, you're essentially doing the same thing o1 does - just on a smaller scale. So when you hit a tricky problem, you can use these techniques to nudge any model in that direction. And if you're dealing with something that really needs structured, careful thinking, that's when you might want to use o1 or similar models that are specifically designed for this kind of deep reasoning.

Breaking Down Complex Prompts

When dealing with bigger challenges, I've found these scoping techniques invaluable:

Sometimes a problem is just too big or complex for a single prompt. That's when I use prompt splitting - breaking the challenge into smaller pieces that the AI can handle one at a time. It's like the old saying "How do you eat an elephant? One bite at a time." For example, if you're trying to solve a complex business problem, you might break it down using MECE (Mutually Exclusive, Collectively Exhaustive) categories. You could split it into market analysis, financial impact, operational considerations, and people aspects - then tackle each piece separately with the AI before bringing it all together.

Prompt build-up is about starting at a high level and gradually increasing detail and granularity. Let's say you need to write a complex report. Instead of diving straight into the details, you might start by aligning with the AI on the overall problem and scope. Once that's clear, you work with the AI to create an outline. With the outline agreed upon, you can then move into drafting sections, getting more detailed at each step. This structured approach helps ensure you're building on solid foundations.

And then there's prompt restart, which is really about managing context efficiently. As your chat with the AI gets longer, the context becomes more complex, which can lead to confusion or less focused responses. That's why I often use "compile" (better than "summarize", as then the AI tends to removing a lot of relevant detail) to get a clear statement of what we've concluded so far. Then I start a fresh chat, paste in the compiled conclusions, and continue with a clean slate. This helps keep the AI focused and reduces the risk of it getting confused by too much context.

Understanding Use Cases

The real power of prompt engineering comes from knowing when and how to apply it. Let me walk you through a few categories of prompts I've seen work really well in practice.

Problem Solving

Guidance and decision support is where you use AI as a thinking partner to work through complex decisions. You can lay out your options, criteria, and constraints, and have the AI help you think through the implications of each choice.

Project planning and management involves using AI to help structure and organize projects. It's particularly good at creating project briefs - you can describe your project, and it'll help you think through goals, scope, timeline, risks, and deliverables. I've found this especially helpful as a starting point that you can then adjust based on your specific needs.

Ideation and brainstorming is where AI really shines - it's actually stronger than humans at generating lots of ideas quickly. But your job becomes directing this creativity, making sure the AI stays "creative within the right box". It's like having a super-creative brainstorming partner who needs clear boundaries to be most effective.

Research and Analysis

Information gathering and synthesis helps you find and pull together information from different sources. Tools like

Perplexity AI are especially good at browsing the web to find relevant sources and information for your research.

Summarization and write-ups goes beyond simple summaries. While summarization is useful, write-ups are particularly powerful - you can ask the AI to rewrite a document from a specific perspective or for a particular audience. For example, you might take a technical report and ask for a write-up that focuses on business implications for senior management.

Quantitative analyses helps with numerical problem-solving in several ways. While the AI might not have perfect judgment about numbers in your specific context, it's excellent at helping you structure calculations, create Excel formulas, write SQL queries, and develop Excel scripts. It's like having a technical consultant who can help you figure out "how" to calculate something, even if you need to verify the actual numbers yourself.

Content Production

Text content covers everything from writing reports and articles to crafting social media posts. The AI can help you create first drafts, suggest improvements, or adapt content for different audiences.

Visual content is about using AI to create simple illustrations, diagrams, or mockups. While it's not yet great for polished marketing materials, it's perfect for creating quick visualizations to support your ideas.

Translations and adaptations is much more powerful than traditional translation tools because you can give it specific translation rules. You can tell it things like "always translate this term this way" or "maintain this specific terminology," and it will naturally incorporate these rules. It's also great at adapting content for different audiences or formats while keeping the core message intact.

Communication and Admin

External communications involves drafting and refining emails, proposals, and agreements. The AI can help you strike the right tone and ensure your message is clear and professional.

Internal documents can transform you into that super-organized person who always has perfect meeting documentation. You can quickly create meeting agendas, follow-up emails summarizing key decisions and next steps. It's also great at writing all kinds of policies and SOPs (standard operating procedures). Just describe what you need, and the AI helps you create professional, well-structured documents.

Administrative tasks is about handling routine paperwork and documentation. The AI can help streamline these processes, making them quicker and more consistent.

Learning and Development

Self-improvement turns the AI into your personal tutor for understanding new concepts. It's great at explaining things in different ways until you get it - just be mindful about verification. As mentioned before, a good rule of thumb is that for concepts that appear frequently online (roughly 1,000 mentions), the AI's explanations are reliable.

Coaching others helps you become a better mentor and manager. You can describe a person and situation to the AI, and it will help you prepare for feedback conversations, structure coaching sessions, or write constructive feedback memos.

Team development leverages the AI's knowledge of group psychology and team dynamics. It can help you with challenges like improving psychological safety, making remote work more efficient, or enhancing team collaboration - drawing from extensive research and best practices in these areas.

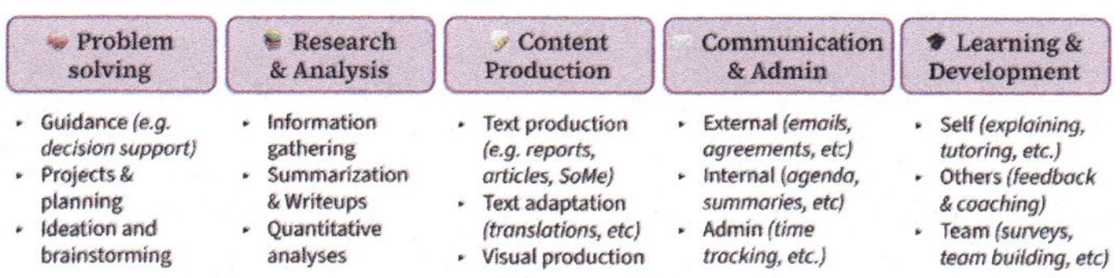

Figure 24. The prompt landscape

However, these are just some examples. The way to find more use cases is to use the metacognition trick of always having a version of you sitting on your shoulder asking: "Is this something an AI could do?" - that way you will find many more examples.

✏️ Exercise: Practice Metacognition & Speech-to-Text

Let's put these key concepts into practice with a real problem you're facing. Take 15 minutes to work through this exercise on your own, an make sure to speak rather than write your prompt:

Prompt 1: Describe Challenge & Request Questions Back

"🎤 I'm working on ***[a problem that you want to solve]****.*

I've already figured out ***[what you already know]****.*

I'm not sure about ***[what you have not yet figured out]****.*

Don't reply just yet, instead first ask me 5 questions for what you need to know to help me."

The **don't reply just yet** part is perhaps the most important, as that makes the hold back on helping out, instead first asking the questions.

Prompt 2: Provide Answers & Request Help

"🎤 Here are ***[answers to some questions]****. Now based on all this, please help with* ***[restating what you want help with]****."*

It's perfectly fine to say something like *"🎤 on question 3, I don't know... make your best guess."* - the AI will make a best effort.

Prompt 3: Iterate (if time permits)

[Ask follow-up questions and refine your approach based on the dialogue]

This exercise helps you practice both metacognition (thinking about what information the AI needs) and using speech-to-text for more natural interaction. Pay attention to how this structured approach leads to better results than just diving in with a basic prompt.

A good thing to know for people who learn prompt engineering is that normal prompt engineering with ad hoc prompts is the first step towards developing skills in agent prompting. This evolution - from ad hoc prompting to systematic templates to agent prompting - is going to be a key skill as we move toward a future with autonomous AI agents.

The Future of Work is Here

Let me wrap up this mini-course with a thought that really drives home why all of this matters. Using ChatGPT as a knowledge worker today is like having a cheat code in a video game. The question isn't whether to use it, but how well you use it. Because while AI won't take your job in the near-term, someone who's really good at using AI just might.

Capability 2: Process Re-engineering

As teams gain experience with prompt engineering, the next step is to transform their collective workflows with Gen AI. This transition doesn't happen naturally - it requires deliberate effort and leadership to move from ad-hoc individual usage to systematic team-wide implementation.

At Ymnig AI, we've helped many teams make this transition, developing practical approaches for identifying high-value opportunities and systematically improving processes. Teams discover unique applications once they start looking systematically - a marketing team might reimagine their content creation workflow, while a development team transforms their code review process, and an HR team rebuilds their recruitment pipeline. Each team brings deep understanding of their domain that helps them spot opportunities others might miss.

We've found that well-documented processes provide a head start for successful Gen AI implementation. When teams have clear Standard Operating Procedures (SOPs) in place, they already have some of the information needed to effectively implement Gen AI. SOPs typically capture the workflow steps and sometimes the decision-making logic.

In this chapter, we'll explore practical methods that any team can use to analyze their current processes and transform them with Gen AI.

💭 Reflect: Process Transformation Opportunities

Take a moment to consider these questions:

- Which processes in your team or organization could benefit most from Gen AI integration?
- What would success look like if you reimagined these processes with Gen AI capabilities?

Your answers will help you identify high-value opportunities as we explore systematic approaches to process re-engineering with Gen AI.

Gen AI Capabilities for Process Change

Before diving into process re-engineering, teams need to develop a deeper understanding of Gen AI's capabilities. This understanding helps identify opportunities and informs how we can systematically improve our processes.

Reusable Prompts

One of the first steps in systematic process improvement is moving from ad hoc prompting to reusable prompt templates.

This transition is crucial because it forces teams to think more systematically about their AI interactions and helps standardize successful approaches across the team.

Looking ahead, one area of prompt engineering that will become more and more important is "agent prompting", and a first step towards that is reusable prompts.

You start with ad hoc prompting - just writing prompts as you need them. Then, as you get more sophisticated, you begin creating reusable prompts with variables as inputs. This is a crucial step because it forces you to think more systematically about your prompts. You're separating the prompt structure from the specific inputs it takes.

Let me show you what this looks like in practice. A typical prompt has three main parts: the context that helps the AI understand the situation, the instruction that tells it what to do, and sometimes example outputs to guide its response style.

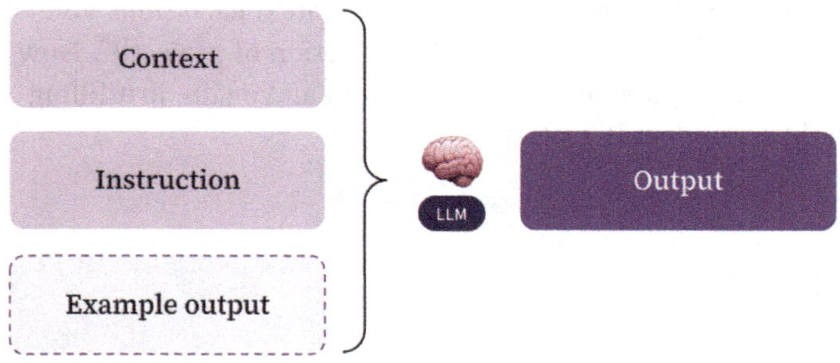

Figure 25. Simplified view of typical prompt

Here's a concrete example: imagine you want to create a LinkedIn post about a successful AI implementation project.

You provide the context (the project results), clear instructions about the post style, and maybe even an example of the tone you're looking for.

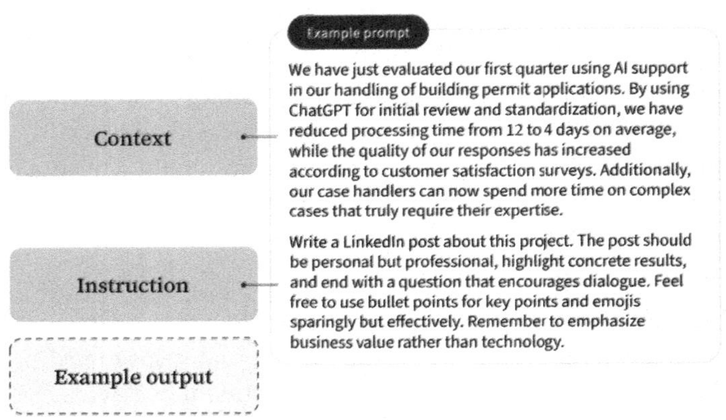

Figure 26. Example prompt

But the real power comes when you turn this into a reusable template. Instead of writing specific context each time, you create placeholders like "{{Brief description of project}}". Now you have a template you can use again and again, just filling in different details each time.

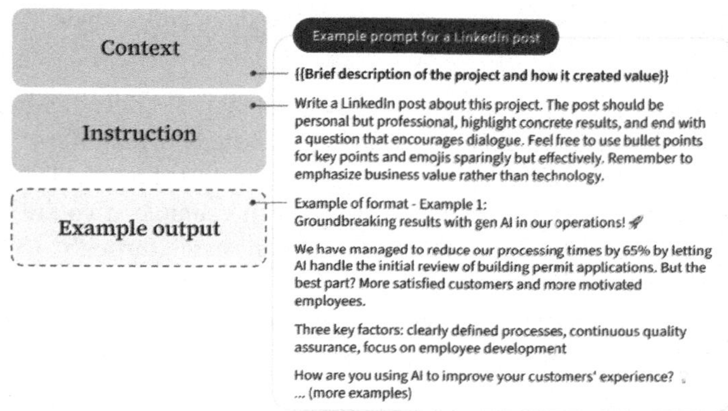

Figure 27. Example reusable prompt

Both OpenAI and Anthropic have tools that make it easier to create reusable prompts. OpenAI's "GPTs" let you build custom versions of ChatGPT for specific purposes without coding, while Claude's "Projects" feature lets teams organize their prompts and knowledge in one place. These tools are making it easier to move from ad-hoc prompting to more systematic approaches.

Applying this systematic approach is the bridge to agent prompting. When you're designing prompts for AI agents, you're creating these reusable templates but taking it further - making them more autonomous and able to handle various inputs automatically.

Retrieval Augmented Generation (RAG)

The next key capability to understand is Retrieval Augmented Generation, or RAG. While basic Gen AI works with general knowledge, RAG lets LLMs work directly with your organization's specific information. Think of it as giving the

AI access to your company's documents, data, and knowledge base.

I've seen teams get really excited when they first understand what RAG can do. Instead of having to paste relevant information into each prompt, you can have the AI automatically pull in the right content when needed. For example, if you're answering customer questions, the AI can search through your product documentation and support guides to give accurate, up-to-date answers. If you're writing proposals, it can pull in relevant case studies and pricing information automatically.

This capability opens up new possibilities for process improvement. Tasks that previously needed human lookup of information can now be handled more automatically. But RAG isn't just about automation - it's about augmenting human work with quick access to relevant information. When thinking about process changes, look for steps where people spend time searching for or compiling information. These are often good candidates for RAG-based improvements.

But it's important to understand RAG's limitations. I've seen teams get really excited about RAG and propose use cases that require analyzing their entire document set at once - but that's not what RAG does best. While RAG excels at finding specific information - like a needle in a haystack - it's less effective at tasks requiring analysis across all your documents. For example, RAG works great for finding what was said about a topic in a specific meeting, but struggles if you want to analyze how frequently that topic has been discussed across all meetings. This is because RAG retrieves relevant chunks of information for each query, rather than reasoning about your entire document set at once. When you need comprehensive analysis across documents, you'll want to explicitly include that information in your prompt's context window instead.

Understanding AI Agents

When teams first start working with Gen AI, they often wonder about AI agents. What can these agents really do? It's important to understand that agents don't have magical new capabilities - they use the same Gen AI capabilities we've already discussed.

As you start working more systematically with Gen AI, you'll find yourself copy-pasting information from one system, putting it into a prompt template you've created, taking those outputs and feeding them into another prompt, checking information in your RAG system, copy-pasting the results into another system, and so on. While this systematic approach works well, it can get tedious - especially when you're doing similar sequences of steps repeatedly. This is where agents come in. They're like digital duct tape and glue - they can connect these different pieces automatically, running your prompt templates, making RAG queries, and moving information between systems without you having to copy-paste.

This is why it's so important to build good process re-engineering skills now, even if you don't have a good agent platform yet. When you create clear prompt templates and well-defined workflows, you're not just making your current work more efficient - you're laying the groundwork for future automation. The templates and processes you develop today can become the building blocks for AI agents tomorrow. So when you're doing process re-engineering, think not just about how to make the process better for humans to execute, but also how it could eventually be handled by an agent. This mindset will help you build more sustainable solutions and get more value from your improvement efforts in the long run.

Identifying Organization-Wide Opportunities

Before diving into specific process improvements, it's valuable to take a step back and look at the bigger picture. I've found that bringing together a management team or cross-functional group to map out opportunities across the organization helps build shared understanding and identify the most promising areas.

The key to successful process re-engineering is focusing on high-value opportunities rather than just interesting use cases. Look for processes that are time-intensive, happen frequently, and follow somewhat predictable patterns. If something is perceived as "boring", that is a strong signal. Also, automating a hypothetical process is much harder than automating a real onw. So make sure you're transforming processes that happen now, have proven value, and clear outcomes.

Start by listing your main business areas and the central processes within each. For each process, consider both the potential for automation (where Gen AI could take over routine tasks) and augmentation (where Gen AI could help humans work better or create new value). Depending on ambition level at this stage, you could also look for areas where you could use Gen AI to do things that weren't possible before, like personalizing services at scale or analyzing information in new ways - just bare in mind that you should start with existing processes to get the hang of it.

You should aim to balance high-level mapping with quick experimentation. While you don't want to get bogged down in implementation details at this stage, I've found it incredibly valuable to do some rapid prototyping of promising ideas. For example, if someone suggests using Gen AI for meeting summaries, take 15 minutes to actually test a simple prompt with a recent meeting recording. These quick experiments help build the management team's intuition about what's possible and where the real value lies. Since most leaders don't have hands-on experience with Gen AI yet, these concrete demonstrations are often much more powerful than abstract discussions.

You're looking for areas where Gen AI capabilities align with business needs and could drive real value. Once you've identified and validated these opportunities through quick tests, you can then select specific processes or roles for detailed re-engineering, which we'll cover in the next section.

A systematic approach to identifying opportunities allows you to prioritize based on potential impact rather than just technical feasibility. The goal should be to start with the areas where Gen AI can create most value, and work from there.

🌍 Real World Example: The "Invisible Assistant" Workshop Approach

One of our customers, a professional organization, found a creative way to help teams identify Gen AI opportunities without getting caught up in technical details. Before introducing AI tools, they ran workshops where they asked a simple question: "If you had an assistant who could help with your daily work, what would you want them to do?"

This framing helped team members identify pain points and repetitive tasks without worrying about whether AI could handle them. One group that frequently conducted field visits and negotiations generated dozens of ideas for administrative support they wished they had.

"By approaching it from the 'assistant' angle first, we helped people think about their work in terms of tasks that could be delegated," their Gen AI Lead explained. "This created a natural bridge to introducing Gen AI as the solution that could provide that assistance."

This approach proved particularly effective with teams who were less technically inclined, as it focused on their needs rather than on the technology itself. When Gen AI tools were later introduced as the "assistant" they had been wishing for, adoption happened much more naturally.

Scope-Specific Process Re-engineering

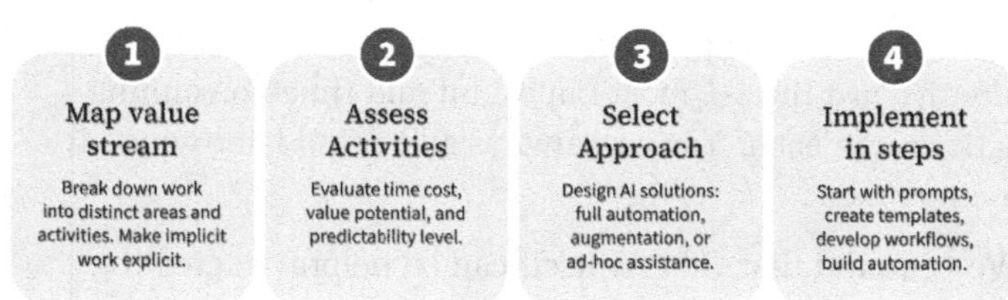

Figure 28. Process Re-Engineering

At Ymnig AI, we help organizations systematically transform their work processes to leverage the power of Gen AI and AI agents. Our approach combines traditional business process re-engineering methods with deep understanding of the capabilities of Gen AI. Here's how to go about it:

1. Scoping and Mapping

The foundation of effective process re-engineering is a clear understanding of your current work. Start by choosing a concrete scope - whether that's a specific role, process, or entire value stream. Break this down into distinct areas of responsibility, then list out the specific activities that make up each area. This initial mapping is crucial because it forces us to be explicit about work that often happens implicitly.

I've seen teams fall into a trap here - documenting every possible variation and exception case. I have seen one process described in 57 slides, some of which with a lot of detail. But process maps that are too complex become impossible to work with. One of my favorite sayings from McKinsey was: "Simplicity is simple. But complexity is also simple. Simplicity beyond complexity, that's the tricky part."

You need to cut through that complexity to find the simplicity beyond, because only then do you have something you can work with. Stay top-down: start with 4-8 main areas, then identify just the 3-5 most important and time-consuming activities in each. You can always add detail later where it matters most.

We've found that Gen AI itself can be helpful in creating these maps - you can describe what a team does and use AI to help generate a structured breakdown of activities. In the case of the 57-slide process description, I gave it to Claude and got a very nice simplified process description.

✏️ Exercise: Process Mapping

Let's map out a work process using AI-assisted Hierarchical Task Analysis (HTA).

1. **Select a Process** (5 minutes):

    - Choose a specific work process you're familiar with
    - Pick something with multiple steps that you do regularly

2. **Generate the HTA** (10 minutes):

    - Write (or speak) a brief description of the scope of the process you want to look at
    - Use this prompt with your AI chatbot: `I want to analyze this work process: [Process scope description] Please help me create a Hierarchical Task Analysis (HTA).`

3. **Refine and Finalize** (15 minutes):

- Use your domain expertise to identify any missing/superfluous steps or inaccuracies
- Iterate with further prompts and manual tweaks until it matches your understanding of the process

This exercise leverages Hierarchical Task Analysis, a technique from the field of Human-Computer Interaction often used by user researchers working on product development, to quickly produce a structured map of your work process. This map will serve as the foundation for identifying Gen AI opportunities in the next exercise.

🌍 Real World Example: Mapping Work Processes Before Ideation

One of our customers, a non-profit organization, discovered that team-level Gen AI adoption was more successful when they helped teams map their work processes before generating ideas for AI applications.

In their early workshops, they had asked teams to brainstorm AI use cases without first documenting their workflows. "We got very limited ideas -

things like 'help us transcribe meetings' - but nothing transformative," their Gen AI Lead recalled. "Teams struggled to see beyond the most obvious applications."

They revised their approach for subsequent workshops, using AI itself to help teams create a Hierarchical Task Analysis (HTA) of their work processes. This systematic mapping helped team members see their entire workflow laid out, making it easier to identify high-value opportunities for AI integration.

"Having that visual map of all their tasks unlocked something," the Gen AI Lead observed. "Instead of focusing on generic AI capabilities, teams could directly connect AI to specific pain points in their actual work processes. The quality of ideas improved dramatically."

This mapping-first approach has now become standard practice in their team-driven adoption strategy, helping teams move beyond superficial applications to more meaningful process transformation.

2. Assessing Activities

For each activity identified, evaluate three factors:

Current Time Cost: How much effort does this activity currently require? This helps prioritize where to focus your transformation efforts. Look at both the direct time spent and any hidden costs like delays, rework, or coordination overhead.

Value Potential: What opportunities exist to enhance value beyond just efficiency? Could you deliver better results, more relevant details, provide more personalized service, or create new offerings? Consider both immediate improvements and longer-term possibilities.

Predictability Level: How consistent and rule-based is the work? Some activities follow clear patterns and rules, while others require significant creativity and adaptation. Ask yourself how hard it would be to express this activity as a reusable prompt.

✏️ Exercise: Task Assessment

After mapping your process with HTA, you'll want to assess which tasks could benefit from Gen AI.

1. **Generate Assessment Table** (5 minutes):

    - Use this prompt with your AI assistant: `Based on this task analysis: [Task analysis]`

```
Please create a table assessing each
task's potential for Gen AI assistance.
Use these columns: - Area (from the task
analysis hierarchy) - Task (the specific
task or subtask) - Assessment (using these
levels): 1 = Fully predictable (clear
```

```
inputs/outputs) 2 = Mostly predictable
(some variation, but probably possible to
automate with an AI agent) 3 = Somewhat
predictable (significant variation, but
probably possible to augment use AI agent
with human in the loop) 4 = Unpredictable
(highly context-dependent, maybe a
human could use an LLM, but not really
an agent use case) 5 = Beyond digital
(requires physical manipulation, deep human
connection, or other non-informational
tasks) - Rationale (explain why you gave
this assessment)
```

2. **Review and Revise** (15 minutes):

    - Check each assessment for accuracy based on your domain expertise
    - Revise as needed, either with prompts or manual edits

The table format makes it easy to spot patterns and opportunities, while the rationale helps you understand the thinking behind each assessment. This systematic approach helps you move beyond intuition to identify specific, high-value opportunities.

3. Select Approach

Based on your assessment, determine the most appropriate implementation path:

For Highly Predictable, Time-Intensive Activities:

- Consider full automation through AI agents
- Focus on standardization and error handling
- Look for opportunities to eliminate manual intervention

For Somewhat Predictable Activities with High Value Potential:

- Design human-AI augmentation workflows
- Focus on clear handoffs between AI and human work
- Build in feedback loops for continuous improvement

For Less Predictable Activities:

- Start with ad-hoc AI assistance
- Document successful prompts and patterns
- Look for components that could be standardized

4. Implement in Steps

Instead of trying to jump directly to the most sophisticated solution, take an incremental approach:

1. Start with ad-hoc prompts to validate your approach
2. Create reusable templates from successful patterns
3. Develop augmentation workflows where valuable

4. Build automation agents for highly predictable tasks

Remember that the goal isn't just to automate existing processes - it's to rethink how work gets done in an AI-enabled world. Sometimes the biggest gains come not from automating current activities, but from redesigning processes to take advantage of what AI does best while leveraging unique human capabilities more effectively.

✏️ Exercise: Implement a Reusable Prompt

Now that you've mapped your process and assessed which tasks are suitable for Gen AI, let's create and test a reusable prompt template:

1. **Select Your Task** (5 minutes):

    - From your task assessment, choose one task rated 1 or 2 (highly predictable)
    - Pick something you do regularly that takes at least a few minutes

2. **Write Your Reusable Prompt** (15 minutes):

    - Gather one or a few specific examples (input and output) of this task
    - Create a prompt template with with clear instructions and output examples

3. **Test and Iterate** (20 minutes):

- Try your prompt template with different inputs
- Note what works and what doesn't
- Make adjustments and add more examples or instructions

4. Document Your Results (5 minutes):

- Save your final prompt template
- Assess how much time it saves compared to doing the task manually
- Note any limitations or ideas for further improvement

This exercise gives you hands-on experience creating the building blocks for process automation. The reusable prompts you develop can later be integrated into more sophisticated workflows or even serve as the foundation for AI agents.

Implementation and Validation

After your process re-engineering workshop, you'll likely have a set of promising approaches - maybe some reusable prompts, RAG implementations, or even early agent concepts. But workshop success doesn't always translate directly to real-world value. I've seen teams get excited about solutions that worked great in controlled testing but required a bit more work to handle the edge cases when in real-world conditions. That's why systematic validation is so important.

Before setting out to improve a process, establish clear validation criteria. What constitutes success? How will you measure improvement? Establishing these benchmarks before implementation helps ensure that you're not just changing processes for the sake of change, but actually delivering measurable value. This validation step also provides essential data for making the case for further Gen AI adoption across the organization.

Start by picking one of your redesigned processes and run it in parallel with your existing approach. This lets you compare results directly and catch any issues before fully switching over. Have the team document when the new process works well and, more importantly, when it doesn't. Look especially for edge cases you didn't consider during the workshop - these often reveal important insights about what needs to be adjusted.

As you validate and refine your approach, gradually expand to more users and more complex scenarios. Build a simple feedback loop - maybe a shared document or regular check-ins - where people can share what's working and what isn't. This helps you spot patterns and make improvements quickly. The goal isn't perfection, but rather steady improvement based on real usage. Once you've validated and refined one process change, you can apply these same implementation patterns to other opportunities identified in your re-engineering work.

Capability 3: Agent Implementation

After exploring AI agents in earlier chapters, it's time to get practical about how teams can actually implement them. This guide is for teams that have identified promising agent opportunities through their process re-engineering work and want to turn that potential into reality. Maybe you've been experimenting with reusable prompts and found workflows that could benefit from automation, or perhaps you're seeing patterns in how your team uses Gen AI that could be turned into an agent.

I'll share what I've learned from helping teams develop and deploy their first AI agents. We'll cover everything from getting your project set up right to managing the development process effectively. The focus here is practical - giving you specific approaches, templates, and best practices you can use with your team. While the broader organizational aspects of agent adoption are covered in Part 4, this chapter is about the nuts and bolts of making a single agent project succeed.

💭 Reflect: Identify Your First Agent

Take a moment to consider these questions:

- What workflow would be good for a first AI agent implementation? Consider tasks that

are repeatable, well-defined, and currently time-consuming.
- What knowledge (documents, SOPs, examples) and capabilities (system access, tool integrations) would an agent need for this workflow?

Your answers will help you identify practical implementation considerations as we explore how to move from concept to working AI agents.

Dual-Track - Rapid Prototype vs Structured Implementation

Before diving into the foundations of agent projects, it's important to recognize that there are two distinct approaches to implementing AI agents, each suited to different scenarios and organizational needs.

The Rapid Prototyping Approach

Modern agent platforms have significantly reduced the barrier to entry for creating functional AI agents, enabling teams to quickly test and validate concepts before committing to extensive development.

When Rapid Prototyping Works Best:

- Simpler use cases with well-defined boundaries

- Processes that don't require deep custom integrations
- Situations where quick validation is more important than perfection
- Teams looking to build momentum and demonstrate value quickly

With this approach, a functional agent can often be deployed in 1-2 days, following a streamlined process:

1. Configure the agent with basic functions and knowledge
2. Test with real-world scenarios
3. Rapidly iterate based on immediate feedback
4. Deploy for immediate value or use insights to inform further development

This approach allows organizations to fail fast, learn quickly, and demonstrate value before investing in more comprehensive implementations. While valuable on its own, a successful prototype frequently becomes the foundation for a more structured implementation as usage expands and integration needs emerge.

The rapid prototyping approach is becoming even more accessible as the market evolves. For teams using platforms that combine AI chatbot and agent capabilities for their everyday chat interactions, the leap to creating their first agent prototype is smaller.

The Structured Implementation Approach

For more complex, mission-critical, or highly customized agents, a structured implementation approach is necessary to ensure reliability, scalability, and integration with existing systems.

When Structured Implementation Is Necessary:

- Complex workflows spanning multiple processes or systems
- Requirements for custom integrations with internal tools
- High-stakes processes where reliability is critical
- Needs for specialized capabilities not available in off-the-shelf platforms

This approach typically takes 6-8 weeks and follows a more rigorous methodology that we'll detail throughout the rest of this chapter.

Finding Your Path

Many successful agent implementations follow a hybrid journey:

1. Start with rapid prototyping to validate concepts and build support
2. Evaluate whether the prototype meets your needs or requires further development
3. Use insights from prototyping to inform a structured implementation if needed

This evolutionary relationship is crucial - rapid prototypes often reveal complexities and integration needs that weren't initially apparent, naturally paving the way for structured implementation. The prototype's success builds organizational momentum while providing valuable insights that significantly de-risk the larger investment.

For the remainder of this chapter, we'll focus primarily on the structured implementation approach, as it requires more detailed planning and execution. However, many of the principles apply to both approaches, and we'll note where specific considerations differ between rapid prototyping and structured implementation.

🌍 Real World Example: Balancing Rapid Prototyping and Structured Implementation

A customer of ours, a professional services firm, demonstrates perfectly how organizations can benefit from both implementation approaches. They use our agent platform for rapid prototyping simple workflows - like responding to internal questions and conducting recurring market research. These quick wins help them demonstrate value and build momentum while requiring minimal investment.

With access to both AI chat and agent capabilities in the same platform, their teams can flexibly choose the right approach for each use case - sometimes starting with chat-based interactions before formalizing these into agent workflows when patterns emerge.

At the same time, they're pursuing structured implementation for high-value processes that justify deeper investment. They're developing specialized agents that streamline their recruitment pipeline and handle time-consuming analysis tasks within their core workflow. For client deliverables, they're building agents that both analyze data and help produce standardized reports - work that used to take hours now happens in minutes. What's interesting is how these two approaches reinforce each other - rapid prototypes can reveal opportunities that later become structured implementations, while experience with larger projects helps identify new quick-win opportunities.

Project Foundation

For agent projects based on the structured implementation approach, establishing a solid project foundation is essential. When organizations start implementing such AI agents, they face a crucial early decision: should they build their agent capabilities in-house or partner with specialized providers? While some organizations, particularly those with strong technical capabilities, might consider building their agent platform entirely in-house, this usually isn't the best use of resources unless you have very specific requirements. Most organizations find more success taking a balanced approach - working with experienced partners while maintaining control of critical capabilities and integrations.

Regardless of which path you choose, there are a number of

elements that make agent implementations successful:

Scope Definition: Every successful agent project starts with crystal clear boundaries around what the agent will and won't do. The most effective approach combines a well-defined minimum viable scope ("the agent must be able to do X, Y, and Z") with a flexible roadmap for future capabilities. This allows you to deliver concrete value quickly while maintaining room for learning and evolution.

Requirements Definition: While scope sets boundaries, requirements clarify how the agent should behave in specific scenarios. Begin with key inputs, expected outputs, and critical constraints, including example scenarios as reference points. Rather than comprehensive upfront documentation, focus on capturing enough to start development while allowing requirements to evolve through implementation and testing. This balance provides direction while enabling discovery through the project lifecycle.

Success Metrics: Beyond defining scope and requirements, you need concrete ways to measure success. This typically includes both quantitative metrics (response time, accuracy rates, cost per interaction) and qualitative measures (user satisfaction, ease of use). These metrics should align with your business goals and provide a clear way to calculate the return on investment. When assessing potential agent projects, focus on ROI rather than simply identifying interesting use cases - the value delivered should substantially outweigh development costs.

Quality Assurance Approach: Ensuring agent reliability requires an appropriate level of quality testing without overengineering. For simpler agents, manual review by subject matter experts might be sufficient to verify outputs. For more complex or critical workflows, a more structured approach with test cases and specific validation criteria becomes necessary. The key is matching your QA approach to your use case's requirements - high-stakes applications need more rigorous validation, while quick-win projects can often use lightweight verification methods.

Executive Mandate: AI agent projects need more than just technical approval - they require clear support and resources from management. This means dedicated budget, allocated team time, and explicit prioritization. The mandate should include not just the initial development phase but also ongoing maintenance and improvement. Without this foundation, agent projects often stall when they compete with other priorities for resources.

Team Structure: Successful agent implementations need the right mix of roles working together effectively. This typically includes:

- A business owner who understands the process being transformed
- Subject matter experts who can validate and do quality assurance on agent outputs
- Technical representatives who can handle integrations
- A project manager to coordinate across teams
- If working with external partners, clear points of contact on both sides

Existing Documentation: Start from well-documented processes whenever possible. Standard Operating Procedures (SOPs) provide invaluable baseline knowledge that simplifies agent development. These documents often contain the steps and sometimes decision criteria and examples that an agent needs to operate effectively. By starting with existing documentation, you can reduce the time needed for knowledge extraction and requirement definition.

Getting these foundational pieces right at the start saves significant time and resources down the line. In our experience at Ymnig AI, projects that invest time in these fundamentals deliver better results with fewer iterations.

✏️ Exercise: Agent Foundation Canvas

This exercise helps you transform promising process improvement opportunities into concrete agent implementation plans.

1. **Opportunity Refinement** (15 minutes)
Building on your process re-engineering work, select your most promising opportunity for agent implementation and refine it by answering:

    - Which specific workflow steps could an agent handle?
    - Are the inputs and outputs of these steps clearly defined?
    - Is this process repeatable and frequent enough to justify automation?
    - Does this opportunity offer significant value (time savings, quality improvements)?

2. **Value & Requirements Mapping** (15 minutes)
Define what your agent will need to be successful:

    - How will you measure success? Define 2-3 specific metrics.
    - What knowledge sources will the agent need (documents, SOPs, examples)?

- What tools or system access will be required?
- Who needs to be involved in developing and supporting this agent?

3. Complete Your Agent Foundation Canvas (30 minutes) Fill in each section of the Agent Foundation Canvas:

AGENT IDENTITY & PURPOSE

- Name:
- Mission:

VALUE & SUCCESS METRICS

- Time/Efficiency Value: *(What time savings will this create and how will you measure it?)*
- Quality Improvements: *(What quality improvements will this deliver and how will you verify them?)*
- Business Impact: *(What additional value will this create and how will you track this impact?)*

SCOPE DEFINITION

- In Scope (will do): *(List specific tasks the agent will handle)*

- Out of Scope (won't do): *(Define clear boundaries)*

KNOWLEDGE & TOOL REQUIREMENTS

- Required Knowledge Sources: *(What information will the agent need access to?)*
- Required System Access/Tools: *(What systems must the agent interact with?)*

IMPLEMENTATION PLAN

- Team: *(Who needs to be involved in development and use?)*
- Approach: *(Starting point and scale - minimal prototype or comprehensive solution?)*

The completed canvas gives you a blueprint for your agent implementation, addressing both business and technical requirements. It serves as a reference document when you begin development and helps ensure alignment among stakeholders.

The Implementation Process

The process I'll outline here applies primarily to the structured implementation approach. Teams following the rapid prototyping path will move through a more condensed version of these phases, often completing in days what might take weeks in a full implementation.

Based on our experience with agent implementations, we've found it useful to think about the process as three parallel workstreams that interact at key points through structured workshops and collaboration sessions.

The first workstream is led by the business team, focusing on requirements definition, validation, and operational implementation. The second consists of collaborative workshops where business and development teams align on objectives and ensure quality standards. The third is the technical implementation by the agent developer team, handling everything from integrations to quality assurance tools.

Let me walk you through how these workstreams unfold across four main phases, following an agile approach that delivers value incrementally:

Phase 1: Information Inventory

The process begins with a mapping workshop (1-3 hours) where business and development teams meet to map the current process and identify critical requirements. The business team then analyzes current workflows and documents key requirements, while the agent developer team sets up API connections, builds data extraction frameworks, and implements foundational tools.

This phase focuses heavily on leveraging existing documentation. In our experience, well-documented SOPs and a good set of reference example outputs often provide 60-80% of the knowledge an agent needs. The remaining information typically comes from discussions with subject matter experts to clarify edge cases and decision criteria that might not be obvious.

Phase 2: Prompt Refinement

About one or two weeks in, the teams collaborate in a workshop (2-3 hours) that focuses on agent prompt strategies, testing different approaches against real use cases and calibrating quality criteria. Following this, the business team analyzes initial results and refines requirements, while the development team implements core process flows, API integrations, and quality assurance systems.

This phase is inherently iterative. No matter how experienced the agent developers are, finding the optimal prompt structure and content requires testing various approaches. The business stakeholders play a crucial role here, as they often have the domain knowledge to recognize subtle issues in agent responses that technical teams might miss. But there's more to it than just reviewing results - I've found that having someone from the business team deeply involved in writing and refining the actual prompts is crucial. This hands-on involvement in prompt engineering helps the business team build their own Gen AI capabilities, which should be one of the goals when developing custom agents. When business teams learn to craft effective prompts themselves, they're much better equipped to maintain and evolve the agent over time.

Phase 3: Practical Validation

After two-three more weeks, the teams come together in a workshop (2-3 hours) to launch the pilot. Before the start of this workshop, the agent developers have developed a working agent. In this workshop, the teams verify solution quality and compare efficiency with existing processes. During the following pilot testing, the business team validates the solution and assesses performance, while the agent development team responds to feedback and updated requirements.

At this stage, it's good to run the agent in parallel with existing processes. This side-by-side comparison not only validates that the agent works correctly but also quantifies the actual time and quality improvements, providing concrete evidence of value.

Phase 4: Full-scale Implementation

After another two-three more weeks, the teams hold a final delivery workshop (2-3 hours) to review the outcome of the pilot, do a formal handover, and to prepare for onboarding more users.

The entire project typically spans 6-8 weeks. At the end of this, the project has typically reached what we call the Minimal Lovable Agent (Release 1). This can be followed by further iterations, depending on the situation.

This structured yet flexible framework ensures that both business and technical requirements are met while maintaining clear communication and alignment throughout the project. The key to success is maintaining momentum through regular touchpoints while giving each team space to work effectively in their domain.

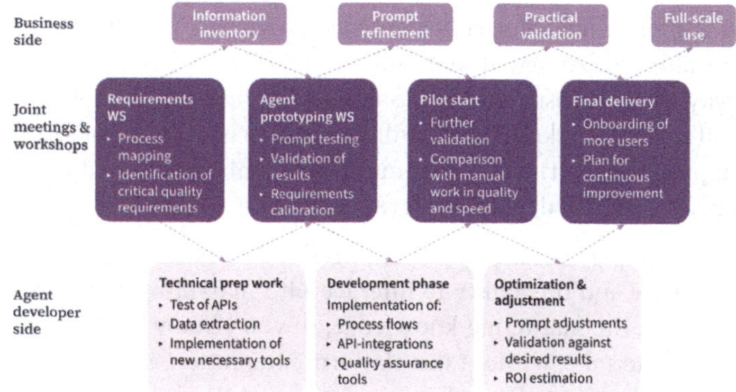

Figure 29. Typical development process for custom AI agent

Tool Development Best Practices

In our agent implementation work, we've discovered that tools are perhaps the most critical component of effective agents. While we often focus heavily on prompts, in reality, about 70% of agent development work goes into building the tools that agents use to take action. These tools define what an agent can actually do beyond just generating text responses.

The following principles apply to both rapid prototyping and structured implementation approaches, though teams using rapid prototyping may leverage more pre-built tools available in modern agent platforms rather than building custom tools from scratch.

Focus on Actions, Not Just Knowledge

The most effective agents combine knowledge with action capabilities. An agent that only has knowledge but no way to act is just a chatbot. Similarly, an agent with tools but no domain knowledge will struggle to use those tools appropriately. The power comes from combining domain-specific knowledge with relevant action capabilities.

For example, a marketing agent needs both marketing expertise and the ability to interact with marketing platforms. Without the marketing knowledge, it won't know what actions to take; without the platform integration, it can only make suggestions that a human must then implement manually.

Limit Tool Complexity

One clear best practice we've observed is limiting the number of tools per agent. With current models, agents perform best when they have no more than 4-6 tools of moderate complexity. Beyond this threshold, agents often start to confuse which tools to use or apply them in the wrong sequence.

This limitation isn't a permanent constraint - as models improve, they'll likely handle more complex tool combinations. But for now, if you find your agent getting confused about which tools to use, it's usually a sign that you should split it into multiple agents with more focused responsibilities.

Design for Feedback Loops

Agents need to see the results of their actions to be effective. When designing tools, don't just create actions that modify the environment - also include tools that allow the agent to observe the changes they've made.

For example, don't just give an agent the ability to write to a database; also give it the ability to read from that database to verify its changes. This feedback loop is crucial for agents to learn from their actions and correct course when needed.

Integration Best Practices

The success of an agent often depends as much on its integration into existing workflows as on its core capabilities. When designing tools, consider:

- Integrating with the same systems employees already use
- Maintaining existing authentication and authorization models
- Preserving audit trails for agent actions
- Designing graceful fallbacks when integrations fail

Remember that for business users, the agent's integration into their daily workflow will often be more important than the sophistication of its underlying AI model.

Modular Development Approach

Complex agent systems benefit from a divide-and-conquer approach. Rather than trying to build one massive agent that does everything, we've found much more success building smaller, focused agents that work together.

While the structured implementation approach benefits from careful decomposition of complex processes, rapid prototyping often starts with a single focused capability and expands incrementally as value is proven.

Start Small and Scale

Begin with the smallest possible agent that delivers clear value. This approach not only delivers immediate benefits but creates natural pathways from rapid prototypes to more robust implementations as requirements and opportunities become clearer.

This approach has several advantages:

- Faster time to first value
- Easier debugging and quality assurance
- Clearer measurement of impact
- Lower risk of scope creep

Once your first agent is working well, you can incrementally add more capabilities or build additional agents that handle related workflows.

Decompose Complex Processes

When faced with a complex process, look for natural break points where you can divide it into distinct sub-processes. Each of these can potentially become its own agent with clear handoffs between them.

For example, rather than building one massive agent that handles the entire sales process, you might create separate agents for lead qualification, meeting scheduling, proposal generation, and follow-up management.

This modular approach not only makes development more manageable but also creates more reliable systems, as each component can be thoroughly tested and optimized independently.

Incremental Implementation Strategy

For each agent project, follow this incremental approach:

1. Start with manual prompts to validate your approach
2. Create reusable templates once you see what works
3. Build automation only after you've proven the value

This stepwise approach helps you avoid over-engineering while ensuring your agents actually solve real problems. It also makes it easier to get stakeholder buy-in because you can show results at each stage.

Making It Work

In our agent implementation experience, we've identified several common challenges and their solutions that can help teams deliver successful projects.

Integrate the Knowledge of Domain Experts

Many teams underestimate the importance of domain knowledge in agent performance. An agent with the right knowledge but simple tools often outperforms a sophisticated agent with limited domain understanding.

Invest time in properly extracting and structuring the knowledge your agent needs by working directly with domain experts. These are the people who actually do the work and understand all the nuances that might not be captured in formal documentation. Without their input, you risk building an agent that misses crucial details that make the difference between success and failure.

This knowledge extraction includes:

- Process documentation and SOPs (with expert interpretation of how they're actually applied)
- Decision criteria and edge case handling (including the unwritten rules experts follow)
- Example scenarios with expected outcomes (validated by people who handle these scenarios daily)
- Common pitfalls and their solutions (based on real experience, not just theory)

When domain experts actively participate in shaping the agent's instructions and prompts, they transfer their practical know-how directly into the system. This ensures the agent incorporates both documented processes and the practical wisdom that makes experts effective.

When done properly, this knowledge extraction pays dividends throughout the agent's lifecycle.

Human in the Loop for Critical Agents

For mission-critical processes where errors could have significant consequences, start with human oversight. Design your agent workflow to generate recommendations or draft outputs that a human reviewer can approve before execution.

As the agent proves itself reliable over time, you can gradually reduce the oversight. This approach builds trust while providing a safety net during the learning phase.

Iterative Development and Testing

Agent development is inherently experimental. The team that tests the most variations of prompt structure, tool design, and workflow patterns will typically produce the best results.

When your agent underperforms, don't just tweak the existing approach - try multiple alternative designs and compare them side by side. This parallel experimentation often reveals insights that sequential improvements would miss.

Change Management at Team Level

Even the best-designed agent will fail if the team doesn't adopt it. Include these elements in your implementation plan:

- Clear communication about the agent's purpose and limitations
- Training for team members who will work with the agent
- Regular feedback sessions to capture improvement ideas
- Celebration of early wins to build momentum

By treating agent adoption as a change management challenge rather than just a technical implementation, you dramatically increase your chances of success.

The journey of implementing AI agents is as much about building team capabilities as it is about the technology itself. Each successful implementation teaches your organization valuable lessons that make future projects easier. By following these structured approaches while remaining adaptable to your specific context, you can navigate the challenges of agent implementation and capture the substantial benefits they offer.

Organizations will likely benefit from both the rapid prototyping and structured implementation approaches at different times and for different use cases. The key is matching your approach to your specific needs, constraints, and the complexity of the problem you're solving. Simple, focused agents may be deployed quickly through rapid prototyping, while complex, mission-critical systems will benefit from the rigor of a structured implementation.

Part 4: Orchestrating a Gen AI Transformation

So far, we've explored how organizations progress through different maturity levels with Gen AI, from individual usage of AI chatbots through to integrated human-AI teams. We've seen how teams can drive their own adoption forward through prompt engineering, process re-engineering, and agent implementation. Now, let's examine how to orchestrate this transformation at an organizational level while encouraging and supporting team-level progress.

The scope of this orchestration effort varies significantly by organization size. Smaller organizations might focus primarily on enabling team-level adoption, with lighter coordination needs. Larger organizations typically require more structured transformation programs to drive systematic adoption across divisions and departments. Regardless of size, success requires attention to the drivers that enable effective transformation.

Before diving into how organizations can successfully transform with Gen AI, let me share what I've learned about this transformation and why it is so different from others we've seen before.

A People-Centered Transformation

When I talk to organizations about adopting Gen AI, they often try to use the same playbooks they've used before - like the ones they used for their digital transformation or for implementing machine learning. But I've found that Gen AI transformation is fundamentally different - it's much more about how people adapt and learn than about implementing complex technical systems.

When companies go digital, they usually need to do a lot of technical work up front. The tech or IT teams centrally drive most of the work. They need to plan everything centrally and set up all the systems and infrastructure. While it's important that the people who actually work with these processes are involved in figuring out how to digitize them, it's still mostly driven by the IT department and costs a lot to get started.

Machine learning is even more centralized. You need to collect tons of data first, clean it all up, and then build models for specific use cases. The end users barely get involved - they just get told "here's your model, use it like this." It's very technical and often quite expensive to get going (though costs have come down quite a bit lately).

But Gen AI? It completely flips this on its head. The technology is ready to use right now, and it doesn't cost much to get started. What really matters is how people learn to use it and adapt to it. Instead of everything being driven from the top down, success comes from people throughout the organization discovering useful ways to use these tools.

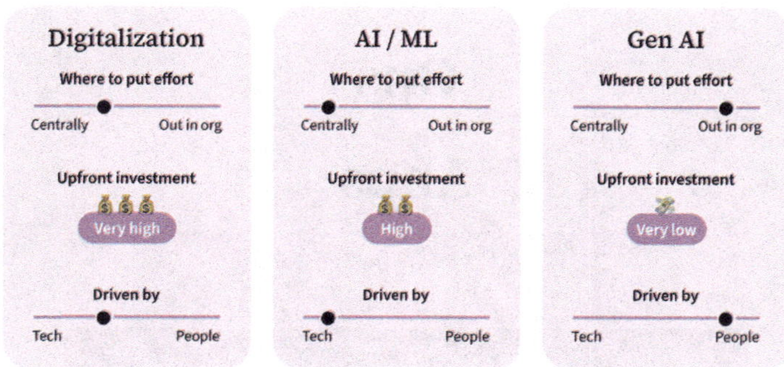

Figure 30. Comparing Transformations

Why is this possible? The answer lies in how Gen AI has evolved differently from earlier AI approaches.

When we talk about working with AI, we typically think about four different layers:

1. Hardware - The actual computers and infrastructure
2. Models - The AI algorithms that do the work
3. Applications - The software that puts these models to use
4. Operations - How people actually use the technology day-to-day

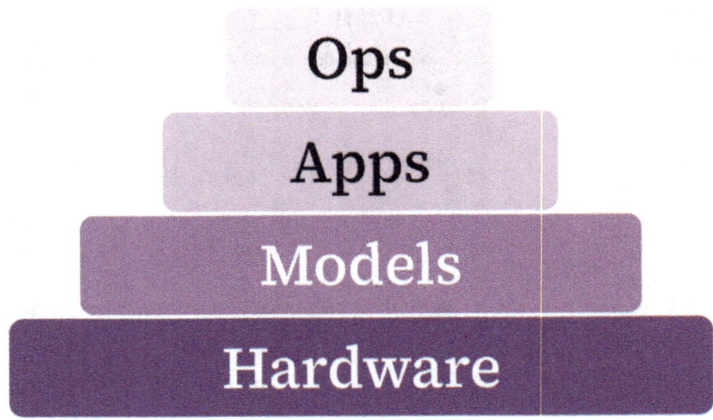

Figure 31. The AI Stack

Before ChatGPT launched in late 2022, when people talked about "AI", they primarily meant Machine Learning, or "ML". This means gathering lots of data related to a specific use case, and having really smart data scientists work with this "big data" to train a model that can be used for a specific narrow use case. Companies had to invest heavily in layers 2-4 (with hardware available in the cloud), from building models to hiring specialized teams. It was very centralized and tech-heavy, and you had to spend a lot of money before seeing any real benefits.

But Gen AI has completely changed this picture. The really powerful foundation models - like the GPT and Claude families of models - are already built and ready to use. You don't need to build your own AI models from scratch anymore. The "models" layer has basically been solved by the big AI labs, which means companies can focus mainly on building applications and figuring out how to use these tools effectively. This makes AI much more accessible to everyone in the organization, not just the technical teams.

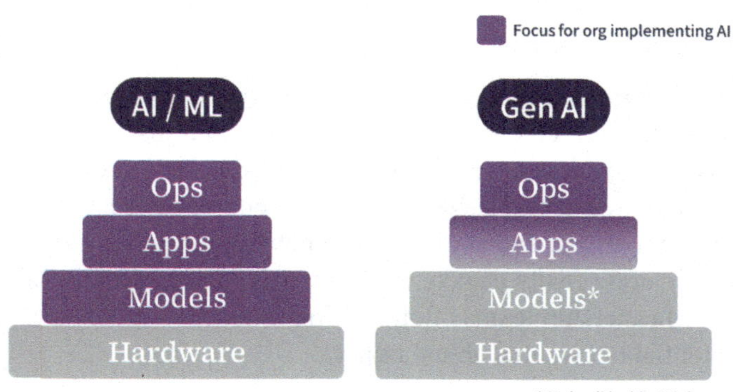

Figure 32. ML vs Gen AI

This fundamental shift in accessibility means that Gen AI transformation can - and should - unfold quite differently from previous technology transformations. Even though adopting Gen AI needs different approaches, that work can happen alongside your other digital projects. The key is understanding that success comes from enabling and supporting widespread learning and experimentation, not from centralized technical implementation.

The Transformation Journey

Through working with many organizations on their Gen AI journeys, I've observed clear patterns in how adoption typically unfolds. Most organizations start in what we call the "wet blanket" phase - where concerns about security and risk create an environment where Gen AI usage is either explicitly or implicitly discouraged. Even when there's no official policy against it, the uncertainty about what's allowed often prevents meaningful adoption. Some people might experiment on their own, but there's no coordinated effort to capture value from these tools.

The first real progress happens when organizations grant access to basic Gen AI tools like ChatGPT. But just providing access isn't enough - many organizations find themselves disappointed at this stage. While some enthusiastic early adopters dive in and start seeing benefits, the majority of people don't really engage with the tools in any meaningful way. Leadership teams often feel frustrated, seeing lots of potential but limited actual impact.

Real momentum builds when teams start actively exploring what they can do with Gen AI. They learn prompt engineering, discover opportunities to use AI in their work, and begin adapting their processes to make the most of these capabilities. In proactive and tech-savvy organizations with very strong learning cultures, this exploration can spread naturally as teams share their successes. But most organizations need a more deliberate approach to drive this learning journey effectively.

The most advanced organizations move beyond individual experimentation to systematic implementation. They help their teams reimagine work processes and develop custom AI agents for specific time-consuming tasks. This is where the real impact starts showing - teams transform their collective workflows around Gen AI capabilities, deploy purpose-built AI coworkers and begin exploring how humans and AI can coordinate effectively as unified teams.

It has been fascinating to see how this journey has played out in Sweden, where I'm based. I've noticed that our strong culture of following rules and ensuring quality - usually a great strength - often slows us down in adopting Gen AI. Many Swedish organizations get stuck in the wet blanket stage because using AI feels like "cheating" when there aren't clear rules about it. Quite a few have made it to providing basic tool access, but are often limited from using the best tools available. Some forward-thinking organizations have pushed into active learning and experimentation.

No teams I know of have reached the fully integrated human-AI teams of Level 4 yet, but some organizations are making impressive progress. Klarna, for example, has reached Level 3 maturity in some teams. Their CEO Sebastian Siemiatkowski has been a strong champion for Gen AI adoption. They were early movers, partnering with OpenAI, and have seen big results. Today, 87% of their people use Gen AI daily, and their AI handles most customer service chats. They're saving $10 million yearly in marketing alone. They've built a real AI culture - encouraging experiments, budgeting for mistakes, and even rating staff on AI use. This shows what's possible when an organization fully commits to a Gen AI transformation.

Driving the Transformation

Through working with many organizations on their Gen AI journeys, we've identified six drivers that determine transformation success. Let's examine how each driver supports progress through the maturity levels we explored earlier:

Driver 1: Urgency While many organizations feel urgency around basic AI chatbot adoption (Level 1), real transformation requires building urgency around the full potential of AI coworkers (Levels 3 and 4). Leadership teams need to understand both the immediate productivity gains from AI chatbots and the transformative potential of AI agents handling complex workflows independently.

Driver 2: Coalition Building the right coalition means enlisting a core team with a strong Gen AI sponsor and lead, plus champions spread across the organization. You also need functional support for access to tools and learning. You then need to grow this coalition over time - from an initial group of enthusiasts to broad ownership across the organization.

Driver 3: Access Organizations need a dual-track approach to access. First, enabling broad access to AI chatbots with appropriate controls (Levels 1-2). Second, developing frameworks for deploying and managing AI agents as you advance toward Levels 3-4. Early consideration of agent governance helps avoid creating barriers to progress later.

Driver 4: Learning Learning needs evolve as organizations advance through maturity levels. Individual prompt engineering skills form the foundation (Level 1), leading to team-level capabilities in process re-engineering (Level 2), and eventually to sophisticated skills in agent development and orchestration (Levels 3-4). Your learning strategy needs to support this progression.

Driver 5: Strategy Effective Gen AI strategy requires balancing immediate opportunities with longer-term transformation. While capturing quick wins from AI chatbots builds momentum, your strategy needs to prepare for the more fundamental changes that come with AI agents and human-AI teams.

Driver 6: Scale Scaling happens across all maturity levels through three key elements:

- Strategic orchestration: Coordinating initiatives and tracking progress
- Innovation empowerment: Supporting team-led experimentation and adoption

- Change enablement: Building capabilities and addressing concerns

This scaling effort complements the team-driven adoption we explored in Part 3, creating organization-wide momentum while supporting local innovation.

In the chapters that follow, we'll examine each of these drivers in detail, providing practical guidance for orchestrating your Gen AI transformation. We'll start with building the critical sense of urgency needed to drive meaningful change.

Driver 1: Urgency

In my work helping organizations adopt generative AI, I've noticed that the single biggest factor determining early success is whether there's a real sense of urgency driving the transformation. Without that urgency, initiatives tend to stall - caught in endless policy discussions or being held back by too much caution.

In this chapter, I want to share what I've learned about building that crucial sense of urgency requires three key elements: a compelling story about why action is needed now, the right trusted relationships with senior leaders, and concrete demonstrations that break through existing mental models.

Why Urgency Matters

Let me start by explaining what typically happens without sufficient urgency. Organizations often get stuck in what I call the "wet blanket" phase - where concerns about security, privacy, and risk lead to policies so restrictive that meaningful adoption becomes impossible. IT and Legal departments, doing their jobs to protect the organization, create barriers that effectively shut down experimentation and learning.

This cautious approach might seem prudent, but it creates a dangerous situation. While your organization carefully evaluates risks and crafts perfect policies, competitors are learning, experimenting, and building crucial capabilities. By the time you're ready to move forward, they may have an insurmountable lead.

And, from the perspective of the cautious IT professional, too strict policies encourage employees to de facto bypass the policy and use whatever tool they deem useful anyway.

The key to breaking through this paralysis is creating enough urgency - particularly with senior leadership - to drive action despite the natural inclination toward caution. When leadership truly understands the stakes involved, they ensure that legitimate concerns about risk are balanced against the very real risk of falling behind.

💭 Reflect: Your Organization's Gen AI Urgency

Take a moment to consider these questions:

- What does the sense of urgency look like around Gen AI in your organization?
- Where do you see the biggest opportunities related to Gen AI?

Your answers will help you better relate to the concepts we'll explore next and identify where you might need to focus your efforts in creating urgency.

Creating Real Urgency

When working with senior leadership teams to build urgency around Gen AI transformation, I've found that success comes from combining three critical elements. First, you need to build trusted relationships that help you ensure your message lands. Second, you need a compelling story that makes the case for immediate action. And third, you need concrete demonstrations that help break through outdated mental models about what AI can do.

Let me walk you through how these elements work together to create the momentum you need for meaningful transformation.

Building Trust with Senior Leaders

When it comes to building urgency around Gen AI, I've found that having a compelling story isn't enough - you need to first get in the room with the right people and have them trust you enough to really listen. Let me share what I've learned about making this happen.

One pattern I often see is Gen AI Leads struggling to reach and convince their CEOs directly. Sometimes you need to build support step by step - first convincing one senior leader, then working with them to convince others, gradually building momentum until you can make the case to the CEO.

> **🌍 Real World Example: Building Support Step by Step**
> I remember working with one Gen AI Lead who mapped out a careful path: first getting the CIO, then working together to convince the COO, and finally presenting jointly to the CEO. This

methodical approach worked much better than trying to go straight to the top.

A framework I've found really helpful for thinking about building trust is called the Trust Equation. It breaks trust down into four components: Credibility × Reliability × Intimacy ÷ Self-orientation. When you're trying to build urgency for Gen AI transformation, each component matters in different ways:

- **Credibility** comes from your expertise and knowledge about Gen AI. This is where having a Gen AI expert involved can be really valuable - someone who can speak authoritatively about the technology and its implications.
- **Reliability** is about consistently delivering on what you promise. This often means starting small, making specific commitments, and following through perfectly.
- **Intimacy** refers to the safety people feel when sharing their real concerns and hopes with you. This is where existing relationships within the organization become crucial.
- **Self-orientation** is about showing that you're focused on the organization's success, not just pushing your own agenda.

What I've seen work best is bringing these elements together through the right combination of people. Instead of trying to build urgency alone, create a small coalition. For example, you might have:

- The Gen AI Lead who understands the organization and can coordinate efforts
- A Gen AI expert who brings deep technical credibility
- A Gen AI sponsor, a respected senior leader who believes in Gen AI and has strong relationships with the top leadership team

When these three roles work together to make the case for Gen AI transformation, you get a powerful combination of expertise, organizational knowledge, and trusted relationships. I've seen this approach break through where individual efforts failed.

Remember - building trust takes time, but it's worth investing in. Without trust, even the most compelling arguments about Gen AI's potential might fall flat. With trust, you create the foundation for real transformation.

The Most Compelling Case for Action

Through working with many organizations, I've found that there's a specific story that helps people understand why immediate action is crucial. It has five key parts that build on each other to create a compelling case for urgency. Let me walk you through each part.

1. Significant Impact from AI Chatbots

As we saw in Part 1, Gen AI is already delivering real value. Studies show that knowledge workers using ChatGPT properly can save several hours each week on tasks like writing, research, and analysis. And these gains are just from basic AI chatbots, the simplest form of the technology.

2. AI Chatbots are Evolving into AI Coworkers

What makes this moment truly pivotal is how quickly we're moving from simple chatbots to true AI coworkers. As we explored in Part 1, Gen AI capabilities are advancing rapidly across multiple fronts - from better reasoning and multimodal interactions to increasingly sophisticated agentic behavior.

This isn't just theoretical progress. We're already seeing early AI coworkers that can handle complex tasks independently, like monitoring technology stacks, screening business opportunities, or managing email workflows. Every other month brings new breakthroughs that expand what's possible.

3. Impact of AI Coworkers will be huge

Looking ahead, the potential impact is enormous. Imagine every employee in your organization having several AI coworkers handling routine tasks, gathering information, and helping produce better work. This isn't just about doing existing work faster - it's about fundamentally expanding what's possible.

The organizations that embrace this potential will see their teams become dramatically more productive. As we discussed in Part 1, when humans orchestrate teams of AI coworkers, their productivity doesn't just improve incrementally - it multiplies several times over. This creates massive competitive advantages for early adopters.

4. Learning to collaborate with AI Takes Time

However, capturing this potential isn't something that happens overnight. It requires building new capabilities across your organization, and this takes time. There are two crucial learning curves to navigate:

First is the "how" to use AI effectively. This starts with mastering prompt engineering but evolves toward what we might call "agent prompting" and "agent orchestration" - learning to coordinate multiple AI coworkers effectively.

Second is the "when" and "for what" to use AI. This means developing new intuitions about when to delegate to AI, how to adapt workflows, and how to make AI collaboration a natural part of daily operations. Most organizations underestimate how long it takes to build these capabilities.

Importantly, the skills we build now with AI chatbots form the foundation for working with more advanced systems later. And since there's no sharp transition point from chatbots to coworkers - it's a gradual evolution - waiting for some clear moment to start will inevitably leave you behind.

5. The Imperative to Act

Let me recapitulate the core components of the argument:

1. We already know that current AI chatbots deliver real value - helping people save several hours each week.
2. We're seeing these tools evolve from simple chatbots into true AI coworkers that can handle complex tasks independently.

3. In the future, we'll work with many such AI coworkers, which will make us many times more productive than we are today.
4. Working effectively with Gen AI isn't something you learn overnight - it's a continuous learning journey that builds over time.

If we sum this up, it brings us to the conclusion: **Organizations that start learning how to work with AI now will have a competitive advantage as AI capabilities continue to improve**.

The learning curve is steep, and the gap between leaders and laggards will widen over time. Those who push for this now will be the future winners. Therefore, organizations need to start their Gen AI journey now.

During 2025, we'll see ever more sophisticated AI coworkers becoming a reality. Organizations that have spent more time learning and adapting will be better prepared to leverage these capabilities effectively. Those that haven't may find themselves far behind, struggling to catch up.

Regional Variations in Gen AI Adoption

Different regions are adopting Gen AI at vastly different rates, creating potential competitive gaps. Let me share a specific example from my home country of Sweden, which illustrates what can happen when a traditionally tech-forward country falls behind:

A 2025 study by Boston Consulting Group, "GenAI in the Nordics: A deep-dive on Sweden", reveals a stark adoption gap between Sweden and other countries:

- Only 18% of Swedish white-collar workers report using Gen AI weekly, compared to 54% in Europe and 61% globally – a 36 percentage point gap
- Nordic Gen AI users report far less benefit: 2.6 hours of weekly time savings versus 5.3 hours for European users - and the factor that makes the biggest in time savings is whether user received training

This pattern is particularly concerning for Sweden, which traditionally sees itself as a technology leader. Carl-Henric Svanberg, who led Sweden's AI Commission, recently warned that Sweden has fallen behind in AI development. "Swift and decisive action is needed to catch up," he emphasized, highlighting the urgency for Swedish organizations to accelerate their AI adoption.

This pattern – where even traditionally strong tech regions can fall behind – underscores a crucial point: no organization can take their position for granted in the Gen AI race. Those who delay action risk finding themselves facing not just a technology gap, but a fundamental competitive disadvantage that becomes increasingly difficult to overcome.

🌍 Real World Example: Building Multilevel Urgency

At a large industrial company, a customer of ours, the Gen AI Lead took a two-pronged approach to building urgency. Rather than focusing solely on executive buy-in, he simultaneously engaged leadership groups through formal presentations and captured grassroots enthusiasm through various forums.

This multilevel approach proved highly effective. While leadership presentations established top-level support and resources, the employee forums uncovered existing pockets of experimentation and enthusiasm. By connecting these top-down and bottom-up movements, he created a much stronger sense of organizational urgency than either approach could have achieved alone.

The Gen AI Lead later reflected: "Creating urgency at just the executive level wasn't enough. We needed both executive sponsorship and visible employee enthusiasm to really drive momentum across the organization."

🌍 Real World Example: Creating Momentum Without Top-Down Direction

Another customer of ours, a global manufacturing

company found itself in a situation where executive leadership hadn't yet provided clear direction on Gen AI adoption, despite growing interest throughout the organization.

Rather than waiting for top-down mandates, their Gen AI Lead focused on building momentum from the bottom up. By supporting early adopters, facilitating pilots, and documenting successful use cases, they created natural pressure for more formal organizational commitment.

"Eventually, we reached a tipping point where there was so much bottom-up experimentation that leadership's focus shifted from deciding whether to adopt Gen AI to coordinating the adoption that was already happening," explained their Gen AI Lead. "Sometimes the most effective strategy isn't waiting for perfect conditions from the top, but creating enough grassroots momentum that formal recognition becomes inevitable."

This approach proved particularly effective in their engineering-focused culture, where demonstrated results carried more weight than executive declarations.

✏️ Exercise: Building and Testing Your Case for Gen AI Urgency

Create a compelling, tested case for Gen AI adoption in your organization through these three steps:

1. **Assess Current State** (30 min) Create a simple one-page assessment covering:

- Current Gen AI adoption level (access, usage, policies)
- Urgency levels across different departments
- Key stakeholders and their attitudes
- Main barriers and concerns

2. **Draft Your Case** (45 min) Create a 5-minute pitch including:

- Core argument for why to go for Gen AI
- 2-3 concrete examples of potential impact
- Clear next steps you're proposing
- Responses to likely objections

3. **Test and Refine** (1-2 days)

- Present your pitch to 2-3 colleagues
- Document their reactions and concerns
- Note which arguments resonated most

- Revise your pitch based on feedback

By the end of this exercise, you'll have a tested, refined pitch for driving Gen AI adoption, backed by real feedback from your organization.

The Power of Examples

When I talk to organizations about creating urgency for Gen AI adoption, I've found that sometimes the most powerful approach is the simplest - just showing people what Gen AI can actually do. Many leaders are still operating with mental models from the pre-Gen AI world, and well-chosen demonstrations can completely shift their perspective.

Let me share the two approaches I've found most effective:

1. Show What's Possible in Their World

The most powerful demonstrations connect directly to the person's actual work. By making it interactive and relevant to their context, you create those crucial "wow moments" that shift their thinking. Instead of abstract discussions about AI's potential, you show them concrete value in their specific situation.

🌍 Real World Example: The Strategic Memo Demo

One particularly effective demonstration I use with senior teams is what I call the "Strategic Memo Demo." Here's how it works:

1. Ask the team to pick a strategic topic they're currently discussing
2. Have them talk through their thoughts for 5-10 minutes while using AI to capture and structure their thinking
3. Generate a one-page strategic memo based on the discussion
4. Get their feedback on what's missing or could be better
5. Update the memo in real-time incorporating their feedback

What makes this so powerful is how quickly you can converge on a memo that truly captures their strategic thinking. In just 15-20 minutes, you can go from loose discussion to a polished document that reflects their expertise and judgment. While this requires prompting skills, it consistently creates those "aha moments" where leaders see the technology's real potential (I've often been brought in as an Gen AI Expert to conduct these sessions, and sometimes prepped the Gen AI Lead). The tools I use for this (at the time of writing) is ChatGPT for voice capture, and then copy-paste to Claude for writing and iterating on the memo.

2. Show Where This is Heading

The second crucial piece is helping people understand the trajectory of Gen AI evolution. I often use the analogy of mobile phones - today's ChatGPT is like SMS in the early days of mobile phones. Just as SMS evolved into smartphones that transformed how we communicate and work, we're seeing Gen AI evolve from simple chatbots toward true AI coworkers.

To make this concrete, I demonstrate two things:

- Recent breakthroughs like OpenAI's SORA model generating videos from text descriptions, showing how quickly new capabilities are emerging
- AI agents handling entire workflows independently, previewing how we'll work with AI coworkers in the near future

When you combine these two elements - showing concrete value in their world today and giving them a visceral sense of where this is heading - people often have that crucial shift in perspective. They move from intellectual understanding to feeling in their bones that this technology will transform how we work. That's when real urgency starts to build.

We'll explore this future trajectory in more detail in Driver 5: Strategy, where we'll use strategic foresight techniques to help you envision different scenarios for how Gen AI might develop in your specific context.

Remember - seeing is believing. These demonstrations can do more to create urgency than hours of presentations and discussions. When people experience firsthand what Gen AI can do and where it's heading, they often shift from "Should we do this?" to "How quickly can we start?"

🌍 Real World Example: Prioritizing Gen AI Amid Organizational Change

A customer of ours, a labor union, faced the challenge of implementing Gen AI while simultaneously going through significant organizational restructuring and staff reductions.

Rather than delaying their Gen AI initiatives until after the reorganization, their leadership team made the strategic decision to move forward with both simultaneously. They recognized that Gen AI tools could actually help employees handle increased workloads resulting from the staffing changes.

"It wasn't an ideal time to introduce new technology," their Gen AI Lead explained, "but we positioned it as something that would make people's work easier during a challenging period. We focused our messaging on how current AI chatbots could help with immediate pain points rather than talking about future AI coworkers, which wouldn't have landed well during a reduction in workforce."

By carefully calibrating their message to focus on practical, immediate benefits, they were able to create urgency around Gen AI adoption despite the competing priorities of organizational change.

From Urgency to Coalition

Let me wrap up what I've shared about creating urgency for Gen AI adoption. Through building trust with senior leaders, telling a compelling story about why action is needed now, and demonstrating what the technology can actually do with concrete examples, you can create the momentum needed for real transformation.

But remember - the goal isn't to rush in blindly. It's about moving forward thoughtfully but decisively. You need enough urgency to overcome excessive caution, but not so much that you skip important steps.

In the next chapter, we'll look at what happens once you've built that urgency - how to assemble the right coalition of people who can drive Gen AI adoption across your organization. This coalition will be crucial for turning the momentum you've created into meaningful action and lasting change.

Driver 2: Coalition

Building urgency with senior leadership creates the foundation for transformation, but turning that urgency into action requires assembling the right coalition. Let me share what I've learned about building an effective network of people who can drive Gen AI adoption across your organization.

💭 **Reflect: Building Your Gen AI Coalition**
Take a moment to consider these questions:

- Who are the key stakeholders who need to be involved in your Gen AI transformation?
- Where do you expect to find enthusiasm or resistance within your organization?

Your answers will help you identify who needs to be part of your coalition as we explore the different roles needed for successful Gen AI adoption.

Creating the Core Team

Building a strong core team is the first critical step after creating urgency with senior leadership. Let me walk through the key roles you'll need: a Gen AI Sponsor to provide top-level support, a Gen AI Lead to drive the transformation, Gen AI Champions to spread adoption across the organization, Gen AI Users who'll ultimately make this real in their daily work, and potentially external Gen AI Experts and Trainers to accelerate your journey.

Your **Gen AI Sponsor** needs to convert senior leadership urgency into active support. This means more than just saying "yes, this is important." You need someone at the C-level who will participate in key decisions, allocate real budget and resources, do regular check-ins to remove barriers, and visibly champion Gen AI initiatives. Your sponsor needs to protect the transformation from competing priorities.

You're also going to need somebody who can serve as a central project manager - let's call this role the **Gen AI Lead**. Almost nobody has real experience leading Gen AI transformations yet, so how do you pick one? I've seen three paths work well: a business/strategy person with some tech background and change leadership experience, a successful Gen AI champion who's shown they can drive adoption in their area, or a change management expert who's willing to dive deep into Gen AI. The key is finding someone who can bridge technical and business perspectives while driving change effectively.

Beyond just the lead, you need more people out in the organization - we'll call these **Gen AI Champions**. In the early phase, look for people who show natural enthusiasm for Gen AI, have influence in their areas, and are willing to experiment and learn. Start small with just a few champions, but pick them strategically to represent different parts of the organization. You'll identify more and build broader momentum later.

Then there are the **Gen AI Users** - these are all the people that should actually use AI tools and agents in their daily work. While they might not be part of your initial core team, it's crucial to keep them in mind from the start. In the near future, all knowledge worker jobs will have a (silent) AI prefix - "AI Marketer", "AI Administrator", "AI Procurement Officer". Not using AI will be as unthinkable then as not using computers is today. This means a major learning effort is needed, and your coalition needs to ultimately expand to include everyone.

Most organizations need some external support, at least initially, to accelerate their transformation. A **Gen AI Expert** can help you understand both the strategic and organizational implications as well as the technical ones. They bring experience from seeing similar challenges across multiple organizations and can help you avoid common pitfalls. **Gen AI Trainers** play a crucial role in building capabilities across your organization through workshops, training materials, and hands-on coaching. The decision on what capabilities to build internally versus getting external help for should be based on your current situation and long-term strategy.

Engaging Key Functions

When building your coalition, you need to think about two types of functional support. First, there's the active support you need to make Gen AI work in practice. Then there's the broader stakeholder alignment needed to prevent roadblocks. Let me walk through both.

Getting Essential Support

To make Gen AI work in your organization, you need two critical things: access to good tools and support for learning. This means working closely with two central functions.

First, you need IT to help provide safe and effective access to Gen AI tools. They need to vet and approve tools, set up proper security measures, and make sure people can actually use these tools in their daily work. IT will usually take the lead on this. The key is to start this discussion early and find a way to balance security needs with making tools actually accessible and usable. We'll dive deeper into how to handle access effectively in the next chapter on Access.

Second, you need support for learning and capability building. This typically comes from Learning & Development (L&D), but I've seen different approaches work. In some companies, L&D takes strong ownership and drives the learning agenda. In others, the data/AI team or even the strategy team steps up to lead training efforts. We'll explore more what I've learned about developing Gen AI capabilities across organizations in the chapter after next, on Learning.

Building Broader Alignment

Beyond these essential partners, you need to make sure other key stakeholders feel involved and supportive. Here are the main groups to consider:

Your data and AI teams are crucial stakeholders, especially if they've been working on traditional machine learning projects. They might see Gen AI as competing with their existing work. I've seen cases where teams hesitate to adopt foundation models because they've invested heavily in custom ML solutions. Help them see how Gen AI can complement their work rather than replace it.

Legal and compliance teams will have their own concerns about data privacy, intellectual property, and regulatory requirements. Rather than seeing them as blockers, involve them early to understand and address their concerns. This helps build trust and usually leads to more constructive solutions.

Strategy and transformation teams need to see how Gen AI initiatives fit with other ongoing changes. If you have a Program Management Office (PMO), make sure your Gen AI work aligns with their framework. This prevents your initiatives from being seen as competing with other strategic priorities.

Business unit leaders are your ultimate stakeholders - their teams will need to adopt Gen AI in practice. Beyond just getting support from your sponsor, you need to help these leaders see the concrete benefits for their areas. This means understanding their challenges and showing how Gen AI can help solve real problems they face.

The key to working with all these functions is finding the right balance. You need enough alignment to move forward, but you can't wait for perfect agreement on everything. Keep the focus on practical progress while being respectful of different perspectives and concerns.

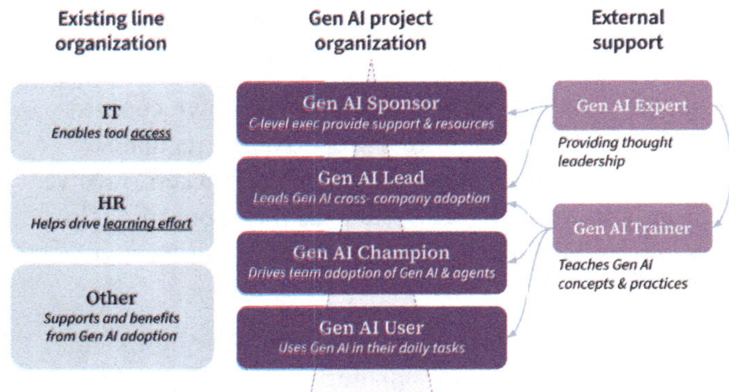

Figure 33. Transformation Roles

🌍 Real World Example: Navigating ML/Gen AI Team Tensions

A customer of ours, a large industrial company, encountered significant challenges when their Gen AI initiatives were initially slowed by existing AI/ML teams who perceived Gen AI as competing with their established machine learning work.

"Our traditional AI teams had spent years building ML capabilities and data infrastructure," explained their Gen AI Lead. "When Gen AI arrived, there was a natural tendency to say 'you can't do anything useful with Gen AI until you have your data structured properly' – which would have significantly delayed adoption."

They addressed this challenge by carefully positioning Gen AI as complementary rather

> than competitive to existing ML initiatives. They established a dual-track approach where ML continued to focus on data-intensive prediction problems, while Gen AI focused on knowledge work augmentation.
>
> "The breakthrough came when we stopped treating AI as a single domain and clearly differentiated the use cases," their Gen AI Lead noted. "Eventually, even our ML specialists began using Gen AI for their own productivity, which helped bridge the gap between these supposedly competing approaches."

Building the Champion Network

Once you have your core team and key functions aligned, it's time to expand your network of Gen AI Champions. Some companies give their champion groups special names - one called theirs the "Gen AI Vanguard" - but whatever you call it, aim for creating a connected group of champions who work together to drive change across the organization.

Creating an Effective Champion Group

Your champion network needs structure to be effective. Start by bringing your champions together regularly - maybe every two weeks - to share what they're learning and help each other overcome challenges. This creates momentum as champions see they're part of something bigger.

What's really powerful is when champions start learning from each other. A champion from marketing might discover a great way to use Gen AI for content creation that sparks ideas for the sales team. Or someone in HR finds a prompt technique that helps the procurement team improve their vendor communications. This cross-pollination of ideas speeds up learning across the organization.

Ensuring Broad Representation

When picking champions, think carefully about representation. You want champions from different parts of your organization - different business units, different functions, different locations. This helps in two ways: it gives you broader reach, and it brings diverse perspectives to your champion group.

I've found it particularly valuable to look for champions in teams that are already moving ahead with Gen AI. For example, in one company I worked with, the marketing team was way ahead in using Gen AI. Their champion became a key voice in the champion network, showing others what's possible and helping build momentum across the organization.

Supporting Champion Success

Your champions need support to succeed. This means:

- Giving them time to experiment and learn
- Providing access to good tools and training
- Creating safe spaces where they can try things out without fear of failure

- Recognizing and celebrating their successes

One particularly effective approach I've seen is having champions document and share their success stories. When a champion figures out a new way to use Gen AI that saves their team hours of work, get them to share that story. These real examples from colleagues are often more powerful than any external case study.

Some champions might even grow into bigger roles. I've seen several cases where particularly effective champions ended up becoming Gen AI Leads, using their practical experience to help guide the broader transformation. This creates a natural career path that can motivate champions to invest in building their Gen AI skills.

🌍 Real World Example: From Core Team to Broad Champion Network

A customer of ours, a manufacturing company, planned to start with a small "core team" of Gen AI champions. However, interest exploded across the organization, and the team quickly grew from a handful to over 20 representatives from different departments.

The team's cross-functional composition proved invaluable. They had representatives from finance, HR, R&D, manufacturing, quality control, and service delivery. This diversity ensured that use cases emerged from across the organization rather than just from technical departments. Having champions embedded in each major function also helped overcome initial skepticism.

"Initially, some departments thought Gen AI wasn't relevant to them," explained the Gen AI Lead. "Having someone from their own team demonstrate practical applications completely changed their perspective. Our finance director initially dismissed prompt engineering as 'something for engineers,' but after seeing concrete examples, she became one of our strongest advocates."

🌍 Real World Example: Volunteer-Led Coalition Building

Another customer, a professional association, took an interesting approach to selecting their first Gen AI implementation teams - they let team leaders volunteer rather than assigning participation.

After introducing Gen AI concepts broadly to managers, they asked, "Who would like their team to be among the first to explore these tools?" This self-selection process identified groups that were naturally more enthusiastic and ready to experiment.

"Having team leaders who volunteered makes a huge difference," their Gen AI Lead observed. "They understand their teams are somewhat 'test subjects' in this process, but they're excited about that role. It creates much better conditions for success compared to pushing implementation on reluctant teams."

This pull-based approach to coalition building helped them identify natural champions while ensuring their early workshops took place with teams who were genuinely interested in discovering AI's potential benefits.

Champion Progression to Agent Implementation

As your Gen AI journey progresses, the role of champions naturally evolves. In early stages, they focus on spreading prompt engineering skills and helping teams reimagine workflows. But the most successful champions don't stop there - they become the bridge to Level 3 maturity by identifying agent opportunities and eventually leading agent implementation.

This evolution makes champions incredibly valuable to your transformation. By investing in their development beyond basic Gen AI skills to include agent capabilities, you create internal experts who can drive the transition from basic chatbot usage to deploying custom agents for high-value workflows.

Organizations that successfully reach Level 3 maturity typically have champions who have grown into this implementation role, developing the technical understanding needed to work with agent platforms while maintaining their deep business context.

Evolution of the Coalition

When you start your Gen AI transformation, your coalition works almost like a separate organization. You have your sponsor, lead, and champions working together to drive change. But this setup isn't meant to last forever.

Over time, your coalition should gradually merge into the regular organization. The goal is that every manager starts feeling responsible for driving Gen AI adoption in their area. What started as a special initiative becomes just part of business as usual.

This means you shouldn't build too much permanent structure around your coalition. Keep it flexible and focused on its main job: kickstarting the transformation and then gradually handing over responsibility to the line organization. In the early phases, don't worry too much about this transition - focus on getting momentum. As you progress, start planning for how your coalition will eventually make itself unnecessary.

✏️ Exercise: Map Your Coalition

Take a practical step toward building your Gen AI coalition:

1. **Assess Current State** (30 minutes)

- Map existing supporters and potential champions
- Identify key function stakeholders (IT, L&D, Legal, etc.)
- Note current barriers and opportunitiesgroup
- Document any existing Gen AI initiatives or experiments

2. **Plan Next Steps** (45 minutes)

   - List 3-5 immediate actions to strengthen your coalition
   - Identify first champion candidates and their potential roles
   - Draft initial engagement approach for each stakeholder group

3. **Create Support Structure** (30 minutes)

   - Outline coordination mechanisms
   - Plan first champion gathering
   - Define success measures

This exercise helps you move from understanding your current coalition landscape to creating a concrete plan for building and supporting your Gen AI champions network.

From Coalition to Access

Let me summarize what I've shared about building an effective coalition for Gen AI adoption. By assembling a core team with the right roles, engaging key functions across your organization, building a network of champions, and planning for how your coalition will evolve over time, you create the human infrastructure needed to drive meaningful transformation.

But having the right people in place is only part of the equation. For your coalition to be effective, they need the right tools to work with. Without appropriate access to Gen AI technologies, even the most enthusiastic champions will struggle to make progress.

In the next chapter, we'll explore how to provide safe and effective access to Gen AI tools across your organization. This means finding the right balance between security and usability, establishing appropriate governance, and creating an environment where people can experiment and learn while maintaining necessary controls.

Driver 3: Access

As we saw in the previous chapter, getting IT involved early as part of your coalition is crucial for enabling Gen AI adoption. Having IT as a partner rather than just a gatekeeper makes a huge difference in how smoothly you can roll out access to Gen AI tools and agents. I often see organizations get stuck in the wet blanket phase, where concerns about security and risk lead to either no policies or policies that are so restrictive that nobody can really use the tools effectively. And when I talk to organizations about Gen AI adoption, one of the biggest early challenges they face is figuring out how to give people access to these tools in a way that supports their progress through different maturity levels - from basic chatbots through to sophisticated AI agents.

Let me share what I've learned about how to break through this and get to a place where people can actually start using Gen AI tools productively.

Breaking Through the Wet Blanket Effect

The wet blanket effect typically shows up in a few different ways. Sometimes there's no official policy at all, which makes people nervous about using any Gen AI tools. Other times, the policies are so restrictive that they effectively prevent any meaningful use. I've also seen cases where organizations technically allow access to Gen AI tools, but the effect of the policy is that people won't use them, either because of real conditions and restrictions, or just because reading the policy makes it feel like those restrictions exist.

What I've found interesting is that these restrictions often come from perceived risks rather than real ones. People often have different standards for AI tools compared to other software. There's this perception that AI tools are somehow riskier because they're "learning" from our data. But let me explain the real versus perceived risks here:

The perceived risk is that AI tools are constantly learning from and potentially exposing our data. But the real situation is quite different - large language models don't automatically learn from every interaction. There's actually a big difference between "training" (where the model learns) and "inference" (where it just responds). Whether your data gets used for training is a choice by the provider, and it's one of the real risks you can actually manage through proper vendor selection.

When you think about it, we trust email providers and countless other services with sensitive data every day. I think we need to apply the same reasonable standards to AI providers: understand the real risks, manage them properly, and then make informed decisions - if you trust the company and they promise not to train on your data, great; if you don't, then look for alternatives.

Another comparison I sometimes make: search engines. Think about how we use Google every day. They collect our search history and so much other data about us, then use it for ads and to train their systems. Yet somehow, we're totally fine with that! I find it very inconsistent to let this happen but then completely block AI tools from use.

Let me be clear - I know these restrictions usually come from a good place. IT and Legal teams are doing their jobs to protect the organization. But here's what's interesting: being too cautious can actually create more risk, not less. When policies are too restrictive, people often start using these tools anyway, just without any guidance or oversight. And when you consider the massive potential upside of Gen AI, it's really worth putting in the effort to handle and mitigate those risks properly.

🌍 Real World Example: Security Policies Creating More Risk

A large Swedish bank implemented extremely strict AI policies, including IP-blocking ChatGPT on all company computers. Their intentions were good - protecting sensitive financial data - but the outcome was unexpected.

Because the bank also had a generous work-from-home policy, many employees simply started using the free version of ChatGPT on their personal computers at home. They would copy work-related content to their personal devices to get help from AI.

This scenario illustrates the risks of overly restrictive policies leading to riskier workarounds. That's often riskier than having clear, practical guidelines that help people use the tools responsibly. Finding the right balance between security and usability is essential for effective AI governance.

Reflect: Access to Gen AI in Your Organization

Take a moment to consider these questions:

- What Gen AI tools are people using in your organization today?
- What are the main barriers to getting people to use Gen AI tools in your organization?

Your answers will help you identify where you might need to focus as we explore the key elements of enabling access.

When it comes to enabling Gen AI access in your organization, I've found there are three puzzle pieces you need to get right. Let me show you how these fit together:

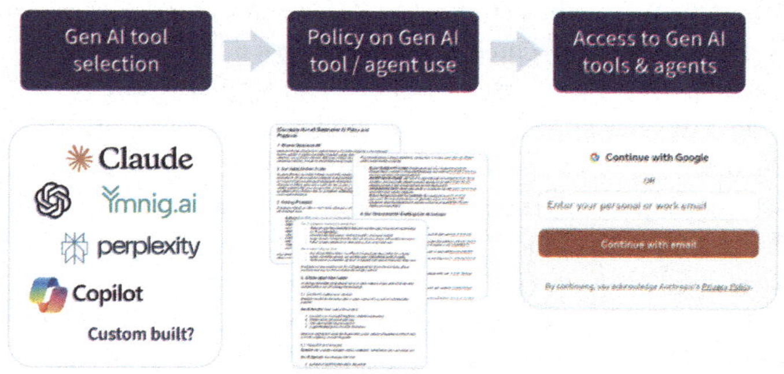

Figure 34. Give access to Gen AI tools

Tool Selection

When I talk to organizations about tool selection, I often see a common pattern that really concerns me. Many companies, especially bigger ones, and at least here in Sweden, just default to Microsoft Copilot because their IT department already has a strong relationship with Microsoft. But this can be a big mistake, especially when you think about where this technology is heading and how your needs will evolve as you progress through different maturity levels.

Let me share a recent experience that really drives this home. My colleague Henrik came back from a workshop where the company only had access to Microsoft Copilot. He was really frustrated and told me, "We can't do this anymore. The tool just didn't deliver the usual 'wow' moments we see with other AI tools. None of my usual examples landed well." The team had to scramble to find a workaround for day two of the workshop just to show what Gen AI can really do.

What's interesting is that I've seen this pattern repeat itself.

While many Swedish companies default to Copilot, I've never - and I mean never - met a team that's tried both ChatGPT and Copilot and preferred Copilot (with similar results almost regardless of which tool Copilot is compared against). Currently, the difference in capability is just too big, even though they're based on similar underlying technology. And this becomes even more important as you progress beyond basic chatbot usage (Level 1-2) toward custom AI agents (Level 3-4). Of course, capabilities evolve quickly in this field, and so this might have changed by the time you read this. Nevertheless, the point remains the same: always evaluate tools based on your actual needs and future goals.

🌍 Real World Example: Choosing Tools That Create "Wow Moments"

A customer of ours, a membership organization had initially planned to focus their Gen AI implementation around Microsoft Copilot, largely because their IT department had a strong existing relationship with Microsoft. However, after attending a workshop where participants used only Copilot, they quickly realized its limitations.

"The workshop just didn't deliver the usual 'wow moments' we were expecting," recalled their Gen AI Lead. "None of our typical examples landed well, and we found ourselves scrambling to find workarounds just to demonstrate what Gen AI could really do."

This experience led them to shift their strategy, choosing to roll out ChatGPT as their initial tool despite it not being the most obvious choice from an IT integration perspective. They recognized that these early "wow moments" were crucial for building enthusiasm and helping people understand the technology's potential.

"We realized that the quality of early user experiences matters more than technical integration convenience," their Gen AI Lead explained. "If people's first interaction with Gen AI is underwhelming, it's much harder to build momentum later."

🌍 Real World Example: Understanding Tool Learning Curves

When rolling out Gen AI tools, another customer of ours, a manufacturing company discovered significant differences in adoption rates based on the tools' learning curves.

During their pilot program with 300 users, they found that Microsoft Copilot required substantially more hands-on time before users felt comfortable and productive compared to other Gen AI tools like ChatGPT.

"With Copilot, we observed what we called 'the hump' – a steep initial learning curve of about 10-15 hours of active experimentation before users started seeing real value," their Gen AI Lead explained. "Most people gave up before reaching that point. With more intuitive tools, there wasn't a hump to get over – it was more like going downhill from the start."

This insight led them to develop different onboarding approaches based on the specific tools being deployed. For Copilot, they created more structured, hands-on training programs that guided users through the initial learning curve, while for more intuitive tools, they focused on use case inspiration rather than technical operation.

Understanding Chatbots vs Agents

As we saw in Chapter 1, Gen AI is evolving from simple chatbots toward more autonomous AI coworkers. This evolution means we need to think about two different types of AI capabilities: chatbots and agents.

Chatbots are what most people are familiar with today - things like ChatGPT, Claude, or Copilot. You interact with them directly, asking questions or giving them tasks one at a time. They're incredibly powerful, but they need constant human direction.

Agents are different. They're AI systems that can work more independently on specific tasks or processes. Think about an AI that automatically handles your email triage, or one that continuously monitors your company's tech stack and creates update reports. These agents don't need constant human input - they can work autonomously within defined boundaries.

Getting to Level 1-2 maturity primarily requires access to good chatbots and potentially some RAG (Retrieval Augmented Generation) capabilities. Many IT departments can handle these needs effectively, either through paid or enterprise versions of major tools or by building simple custom interfaces. But as you move toward Level 3-4 and start deploying custom agents, you'll need more sophisticated platforms that can better support your teams set up and iterate on agents so that are turn out to actually be useful.

The Changing Provider Landscape

What makes tool selection particularly tricky is that the provider landscape for agents will look quite different from what we see with chatbots today. Let me break this down:

First, you have the model providers like OpenAI and Anthropic. They're pushing the boundaries of what's possible with Gen AI. Today they also offer chatbots, like ChatGPT and Claude. Their tools will become more agentic over time.

Then you have the ecosystem companies like Microsoft and Salesforce. They're working to integrate agents directly into their existing software suites. This makes sense - they want to help their current customers get more value from the tools they already use.

Finally, there's an emerging category of agent platform providers. These companies focus on building platforms for developing and deploying agents - whether they're general-purpose agents, agents for specific use cases, or custom agents tailored to an organization's needs.

Strategic Approach to Tool Selection

When selecting tools and planning for agents, here's what I've found works best:

1. **Evaluate Beyond Basic Requirements**: Instead of just looking at security, compliance, and a pre-existing relationship with IT, create a proper evaluation framework. Test the tools with real use cases that matter for your organization. Think about both immediate needs and future agent possibilities.
2. **Consider Cross-System Integration**: Think about how agents need to operate across platforms. Ecosystem companies will naturally focus their agent capabilities within their own ecosystems. For example, imagine an agent that helps create business proposals - it might need to process meeting recordings, draft documents, convert them to PDFs, send emails, and then update your CRM. Limiting yourself to just one ecosystem could make it harder to build these kinds of cross-tool workflows that span your entire business process.
3. **Balance Specialized Tools vs. Ecosystems**: Different tools have different strengths, and it often makes sense to use multiple tools for different purposes. Right now for example, ChatGPT excels at voice interaction and quick responses, while Claude is better suited for complex writing tasks, deep analysis, and handling large amounts of input (200 thousand tokens, or about 150 thousand words, or roughly equivalent to a 500 page novel). It should also be noted that Google's Gemini model can handle even larger amounts of input (1 million tokens). Don't just look at the obvious choices - there's a great website called theresanaiforthat.com that lists over 30,000 AI applications. The right combination

of tools and agents really depends on what you're trying to do and where you want to go.

4. **Plan for Future Evolution**: Start with tools that give you immediate value while keeping options open for future agent capabilities. The chatbots you choose now will impact what agent capabilities you can access later. At Ymnig AI, our platform is especially focused on this evolution - we've designed it with what we call a "low floor and high ceiling" approach. This means users can easily get started with simple AI chatbots (the low floor) but then have a clear path to developing more advanced AI agents (the high ceiling) as their needs and capabilities grow.
5. **Partner Rather Than Build**: I've seen many IT departments pull strongly toward wanting to build their own agents in-house. While building your own agents might seem like it gives you more control, I've seen this approach fail several times. What usually happens is that the IT department gets stuck, causes delays, and then ends up getting external help anyway. Building effective agents requires expertise that most IT departments don't have - both technical AI skills and, even more importantly, knowledge of how to make agents truly helpful to humans. Rather than seeing this as a limitation, the best path forward is usually a partnership - which leads to faster and better results than building everything in-house.

Remember, the goal isn't just to pick the best tools for today - it's to set your organization up for success as we move toward a future where AI coworkers become an integral part of how work gets done.

🌍 Real World Example: Balanced Tool Access Strategy

A customer of ours, a global industrial company, developed a multi-tier approach to Gen AI tool access that balanced security requirements with practical usability. Rather than implementing a one-size-fits-all policy, he created different tiers of tools with appropriate guidelines for each.

For highly sensitive work, they deployed company-controlled tools running on internal servers. For general business tasks, they approved and configured enterprise versions of major AI platforms with appropriate data controls. They also established clear guidelines for when each type of tool was appropriate.

This balanced approach prevented the "wet blanket" effect that completely restricts adoption while still addressing legitimate security concerns. By providing multiple options rather than a single tool, they enabled teams to select the right solution for their specific needs while maintaining appropriate governance.

Creating Balanced Gen AI Policies

The policy piece is the bridge between selecting your tools and giving people access to them. I've found that having a clear, well-structured policy is crucial for successful Gen

AI adoption. That's why I've included an example Gen AI policy at the end of this chapter that brings together what I've learned from working with different organizations.

Let me walk you through what I think makes a really effective Gen AI policy, and why I structured the example the way I did:

Policy Structure and Evolution

I've seen organizations handle their Gen AI policies in different ways. Some combine everything into one document, while others split it into a policy (the rules) and a playbook (the how-to guide).

What I've found works best is to start with a simple, focused policy for GenAI tools with an emphasis on chatbots. This initial policy can be established right away - it's more straightforward because we have plenty of experience with how people use chatbots at Level 1-2 maturity. Then, plan for your policy to evolve over time to include agents as your organization starts exploring Level 3-4 capabilities. I've created an example GenAI policy to help you get started that you can download from our website at https://www.ymnig.ai/genaipolicy

Chatbot Policy Considerations

1. **Commitment to Adoption**: Your policy needs to show upfront that you're serious about making Gen AI work. In the linked example, you'll see sections about training programs, resources, and support systems. This sends a clear message: "We're not just allowing Gen AI - we're actively helping you succeed with it."

2. **Vision and Guiding Principles**: A good policy starts by setting ambitious goals for Gen AI adoption. I've found it works best to balance empowering principles ("explore creative ways to use Gen AI") with cautionary ones ("always review Gen AI outputs"). This creates a culture where people feel confident to innovate while staying responsible.
3. **Clear Use Cases and Examples**: I've included lots of real-world examples in the policy because I've found that's what really helps people understand. When people can see how Gen AI might help with their specific role or tasks, it becomes much more concrete and actionable.
4. **Handling Challenging Situations**: This is where many policies go wrong - they focus too much on what not to do. Instead, I've structured this section to address important concerns (like quality oversight, data security, ethical use, and transparency) but frame them constructively. For each challenging situation, rather than just saying "don't do this", we show how to handle it properly.

Additional Agent Policy Considerations

As your organization starts using AI agents, there are a few additional policy considerations to keep in mind. These build on your basic Gen AI policy while addressing the broader scope and impact of agents:

1. **Decision Authority**: Organizations should empower teams to innovate with agents while establishing clear guidelines for more complex implementations. Consider creating a simple framework that scales oversight based

on agent capabilities and impact rather than restricting which teams can deploy agents. For instance, simpler agents might need minimal approval, while agents with significant system access or decision-making power may require additional review. Establish who can modify agent parameters once deployed and create clear escalation paths for when agents encounter unexpected situations. The goal is to enable experimentation while ensuring appropriate oversight for more consequential deployments.

2. **Operational Boundaries**: Set clear limits on agent autonomy that define the playing field while allowing flexibility within it. Outline which types of decisions agents can make independently versus when human review is required. For example, an agent might independently handle routine data processing but need human approval for customer-facing communications or financial decisions. Document data access permissions appropriate for each agent's function and establish interaction boundaries with external systems. These boundaries aren't meant to restrict innovation but rather to create clear guidelines that allow agents to operate effectively within appropriate parameters.
3. **Transparency Requirements**: Establish documentation standards that make agent operations visible and understandable without creating excessive administrative burden. Implement appropriate logging of agent actions and decisions, with the level of detail proportional to the agent's impact. Define how agent-made decisions should be communicated to relevant stakeholders, especially when those decisions affect other teams or customers. Document the underlying logic and rules that guide each agent's behavior, creating an audit trail that allows you to understand and explain agent

actions when needed. Good transparency creates trust while enabling continuous improvement of your agent deployments.

Think of these as extensions to your basic policy - they become more important as agents take on more significant roles in your organization.

Creating Effective Policies: The Bottom Line

Remember, the goal of your policy isn't to restrict - it's to enable people to use Gen AI effectively and responsibly. When you get this balance right, you create the conditions for successful adoption across your organization. Start with a solid tools policy, and then expand your policy framework as you move into using agents.

Access Management

Now, once you've got your tools selected and your policy in place, you need to think about how to roll out access effectively.

Chatbot Access: Start Broad and Fast

For basic AI chatbots, I strongly recommend getting these into as many hands as possible, quickly. The sooner people start using these chatbots, the sooner they learn to use them effectively.

Keep the evaluation period short and focused on practical concerns like security and compliance. Don't get stuck trying to prove value - that's already well-established. Instead, focus on figuring out how to use these tools effectively in your specific context.

Quick rollout also builds the foundation for future agent adoption. As people get comfortable with AI chatbots, they naturally start seeing opportunities for more autonomous AI support, making them better prepared to work with agents later.

Agent Access: Pilot and Roll Out

When it comes to agents, the rollout approach needs to be different, as there is a learning curve involved in using them effectively. While chatbots can deliver immediate value with minimal training, getting real value from agents requires more preparation and experience.

This is why a pilot approach makes sense. Start with one or a few use cases with groups that can really focus on learning how to work with agents effectively. Let them experiment, document what works, and build up practical knowledge about how to integrate agents into their workflows.

Your Gen AI Champions play a crucial role in this pilot phase. The champions who have already proven effective at driving tool adoption (Levels 1-2) are natural candidates to lead agent pilots. By equipping these champions with additional skills and access to agent platforms, you create a natural progression path that leverages their existing influence and understanding of your organization's processes.

Once you have some success stories and learned lessons from your pilots, you can start rolling out agents more broadly. Use the pilot phase to build momentum. Your pilot teams will help others succeed with agents.

Evolving Agent Management

As agent usage grows in your organization, you'll need to develop more structured approaches to manage them effectively:

1. **Access and Controls**: As agents become more powerful and autonomous, granular access control becomes crucial. You'll need:
    - Role-based access levels aligned with agent capabilities
    - Clear request and approval workflows
    - Real-time monitoring and oversight systems
    - Regular access reviews and adjustments
2. **Cost Management**: Agent costs can escalate quickly, especially with continuous operation and API calls. Plan for:
    - Detailed usage tracking and reporting systems
    - Team and department budget allocations
    - Automated cost alerts and thresholds
    - Regular cost optimization reviews
3. **Deployment Management**: As agent usage grows, you need robust deployment processes:
    - Standardized deployment and testing workflows
    - Clear change management procedures
    - Performance monitoring systems
    - Regular maintenance protocols

Again, the goal isn't to restrict - it's to enable sustainable scaling of your agent usage. Build these management systems gradually as your needs evolve, always keeping the focus on enabling rather than controlling.

✏️ Exercise: Sketch Your Gen AI Policy Approach

Take pragmatic steps towards implementing a good Gen AI policy:

1. **Quick Research** List 3-4 key points for your organization:

    - Which existing policies might overlap with Gen AI use?
    - Who are 2-3 key stakeholders you'd need on board?
    - Which team would benefit most from early access?

2. **Policy Draft** Draft a policy based on the linked example/existing policy, consider:

    - Which parts of the example feel most relevant?
    - What specific use cases would you highlight?
    - What's your biggest policy concern to address?

3. **Stakeholder Testing** Test your draft with a few people:

- Who would you talk to first?
- What's one quick win you could target?
- What's your biggest obstacle to tackle?

This exercise helps you nudge your organization towards implementing a Gen AI policy, without trying to solve everything at once.

From Access to Learning

Breaking through the wet blanket phase isn't just about changing policies - it's about changing how we think about risk and innovation. The organizations that do this well find ways to enable responsible experimentation while maintaining appropriate controls.

In this chapter, we've explored how to provide Gen AI access effectively - from selecting the right tools and creating balanced policies to managing access at different maturity levels. The foundation we've laid here with clear guidelines, appropriate tools, and practical security measures creates the environment where Gen AI adoption can flourish. Remember, the goal isn't to eliminate all risk - it's to manage risk effectively while enabling innovation.

But access alone isn't enough. Once people have these tools in their hands, they need to learn how to use them effectively.

In the next chapter, we'll explore how to drive learning across your organization - helping individuals build critical skills like prompt engineering, supporting teams as they reimagine their workflows, and gradually building the capabilities needed for more advanced AI agent implementation.

Driver 4: Learning

Once you've created urgency and given people access to Gen AI tools, the real work begins - helping your organization learn how to use these tools effectively. Through working with many organizations on their Gen AI journeys, I've found that learning needs evolve as organizations progress through different maturity levels. While some learning activities span all levels, others become particularly important at specific stages of the journey.

💭 **Reflect: Learning Progress in Your Organization**

Take a moment to consider these questions:

- What is the level of usage, learning, and experimentation with Gen AI in your organization?
- What could you do to improve that?

Your answers will help you identify your organization's current learning status and areas for improvement as we explore different learning approaches.

Building Learning Foundations

Before diving into level-specific learning needs, let's look at the key activities that support learning across all maturity levels. These foundational elements create the environment and culture needed for sustained Gen AI adoption.

Lunch & Learn Sessions

Regular informal sessions where teams share their experiences and learnings. They could be over lunch, or at another time. Some companies call sessions like these "Show & Tell". These work great for spreading practical tips and building excitement. It can be showing a good success case where a team used Gen AI, maybe a project where it was helpful or a process that has been improved. It could also be a failed attempt where the team made some interesting learnings that can be shared. The point is to create a culture that celebrates learning.

Training

When it comes to training, I've found that you need to cover both how to use AI and when to use it. Different roles need different kinds of training. Gen AI Leads need broad training covering the full transformation journey (much like what's in this book). Gen AI Champions need to learn how to facilitate learning and drive adoption. Users need focused training for their specific roles. To scale all this up, we have helped organizations with "train the trainer" sessions.

A big part of the training is helping people understand how to change their ways of working and really integrate Gen

AI into their daily tasks. This means going beyond just tool usage to help people identify opportunities, understand best practices, and develop good habits around AI collaboration. It's a lot of training, but it's worth it - this is a fundamental shift in how we work.

Coaching

Training is great to get started, but I've found that people often need coaching once they're actually using AI in their work. They hit roadblocks or have specific questions that didn't come up during training. That's when it's really valuable to have coaching sessions available - whether it's with a prompting expert to improve their AI interactions, or someone who can help them think through how to adapt their processes. These coaching sessions help people push past barriers and keep making progress.

Peer Mentoring

This is where Gen AI Champions really shine. They can provide day-to-day support to their colleagues, helping them apply what they've learned and overcome challenges. It works especially well because they understand the specific context and challenges of their work.

🌍 Real World Example: Multilayered Learning Approach

A customer of ours, an engineering company, created a comprehensive learning ecosystem by implementing multiple complementary formats that catered to different learning styles and needs.

They established "AI Tech Bars" - physical locations at their main sites where employees could drop by for hands-on help with AI tools or to discuss specific use cases with experts. They complemented this with monthly "Learning Community" sessions where broader updates and knowledge sharing occurred virtually.

For teams ready to go deeper, they developed workshop series where groups with similar roles would identify pain points, develop prompts, and test them over several weeks before reconvening to share results. This scaffolded approach helped employees progress from basic awareness to practical application in their daily work.

"Different people learn in different ways," noted their Gen AI Lead. "Having multiple learning formats helped us reach everyone, from the curious beginners to the teams ready to transform their workflows."

Level-Specific Learning

As organizations progress through different maturity levels with Gen AI, they need to build specific capabilities at each stage. Let's look at what learning looks like at each level, building on the maturity framework we explored earlier.

Level 1: Individual Capabilities

At this first level, the focus is on helping individuals learn to use AI chatbots effectively in their daily work. This means building fundamental skills in prompt engineering and developing new habits around AI collaboration. The goal is to help people become confident and effective in their daily interactions with AI tools.

Prompt Engineering Training

As we covered in detail in Part 3, prompt engineering is a foundational skill that everyone needs to develop. This training focuses on helping people communicate effectively with AI systems - from basic interactions to more advanced techniques like few-shot prompting and chain-of-thought reasoning.

The key is to make this training practical and role-specific. For example, marketing teams might focus on prompts for content creation, while development teams might learn prompts for code generation and debugging. We typically combine theory with hands-on exercises, having people work with real examples from their daily work. This helps them see immediate value and builds confidence in using the tools effectively.

Hands-on Projects

Nothing beats learning by doing. Let me share a simple way to get started: project briefs. Whether you already write structured project briefs or not, this is a perfect opportunity to use Gen AI.

Here's why project briefs are such a good starting point: they're something concrete that adds real value, and Gen

AI makes them much easier to create. I do this myself using ChatGPT's voice-to-text to talk through my initial thoughts, then I copy-paste that over to Claude to let it write a nice project brief (and I tell it to make it as a markdown artifact).

🌍 Real World Example: Creating Project Briefs with Gen AI

Here's a rough template for a spoken prompt that works really well for creating project briefs, that I have often used with customers:

"🎤 *Help me write a project brief for* ***[name and type of project]****. We want to* ***[main goal and expected impact]****.*

The key people involved are ***[stakeholders and their roles]****, and we're thinking this should take about* ***[rough timeline]****.*

Some important context: ***[any background info, constraints, or special considerations]****.*

Please write this as a markdown document that includes the important sections a project brief needs. Make it concise, clear and actionable."

Try this as your starting point - give feedback and iterate on the first response you get - you'll be amazed at how quickly you can create a solid first draft of your project brief! For more advanced prompting techniques and examples, check out the detailed prompt engineering guide in the chapter resources.

But project briefs are just the beginning. When you're working on any project, always ask yourself: "Could Gen AI help me do this better or faster?" This mindset helps you naturally discover more ways to integrate AI into your work.

Level 2: Team Capabilities

When teams start reimagining their workflows with Gen AI, learning needs expand beyond individual skills. Teams need to learn how to systematically transform their processes and create shared practices that leverage AI effectively.

Experiments

Structured trials of new ways to use AI, carefully monitored and documented so others can learn from them.

Prompt Libraries

Once the organization gets going with prompting, a good way to turn that into an institutional asset is to create a prompt library, a collection prompts that are commonly useful to teams. This helps avoid reinventing the wheel and ensures consistent quality across the organization. The best prompt libraries I've seen include not just the prompts themselves, but also context about when and how to use them effectively.

🌍 Real World Example: Custom Templates as Onboarding Accelerators

A customer of ours, a large manufacturing

company, planning their organization-wide Gen AI rollout realized they needed to help employees quickly find relevant applications in their daily work.

Rather than launching tools with minimal guidance, they developed a strategy inspired by another company's success: creating a library of custom GPTs and prompt templates specifically designed for different roles and departments before the main launch.

"We saw that when tools were introduced with pre-built, contextually relevant templates, adoption happened much faster," their Gen AI Lead explained. "People could immediately see value in their specific context rather than starting with a blank screen."

Their approach involved identifying common use cases for each major department, developing custom templates with relevant examples, and making these immediately available when employees first gained access to the tools. This significantly reduced the time to first value and helped overcome initial hesitation.

"The key insight was that showing someone a general demo of Gen AI capabilities is far less powerful than showing them a prompt template that solves a problem they faced yesterday," their Gen AI Lead observed. "These templates became conversation starters that drove further exploration."

Process Re-engineering

When you start using Gen AI more frequently, you'll often find that your existing processes could work much better if they were redesigned with Gen AI capabilities in mind. This isn't just about adding Gen AI to what you already do - it's about rethinking how work gets done. In Part 3, we walked through a guide on systematically transforming processes with Gen AI. Start by mapping your current workflows, assess where AI can add the most value, and then redesign these processes to take full advantage of what AI can do while leveraging human capabilities more effectively.

Level 3: Custom AI Agents

At this level, organizations start building and implementing their own AI agents. This requires more sophisticated technical capabilities and new ways of thinking about automation. Teams need to learn not just how to use AI tools, but how to create and deploy them effectively.

Champion Development

As your organization moves toward implementing custom agents, your Gen AI Champions need to evolve their capabilities. Champions who have successfully driven Level 1-2 adoption are ideal candidates for deeper development in agent implementation skills. This typically involves specialized training that bridges business understanding with technical implementation concepts. Rather than hiring new technical specialists with no organizational context, developing existing champions who already understand your processes creates a more sustainable path to Level 3 maturity. Some organizations formalize this through development programs, creating clear progression for champions who want to specialize in agent implementation - which not only accelerates adoption but also creates engaging career development opportunities.

Hackathons

These are focused events - usually a half or full day - where teams come together to experiment with Gen AI on real business challenges. I've found that hackathons work best when you give teams specific problems to solve and have AI experts on hand to help. It's amazing to see what people can figure out when they have dedicated time to explore and learn together. The energy and excitement from these events often spark new ideas that teams can take back to their daily work. An especially good setup for a hackathon is to gather the Gen AI Champions and help them prototype AI agents - this prepares them to lift their teams from level 2 to level 3.

Agent Prototypes

Early experiments with AI agents that can handle specific tasks. This often starts with identifying repetitive processes that could be automated, creating standardized prompts, and gradually building more sophisticated automation. A common pattern we see at Ymnig AI is that we start by helping teams find good use cases and draft prompt templates for those, before teams take over and iterate. Once they get to the point where the prompts work really well, but they are tired of copy-pasting the content to and from their AI chatbot, they are perfectly set up for turning those prompts into an AI agent. In Part 3, we covered a detailed framework for implementing AI agents, including how to set up your project for success and manage the development process effectively.

Level 4: Human-AI Teams

This is where organizations work toward building truly integrated teams of humans and AI coworkers. While we're still in early stages of understanding what this looks like, we can already see some key capabilities that organizations will need to develop:

- Understanding how to orchestrate multiple AI agents effectively
- Learning to lead and manage hybrid teams of humans and AI
- Developing new workflows that optimize human-AI collaboration
- Building skills for effective delegation between human and AI team members

Scaling Learning Organization-Wide

As your organization progresses through these maturity levels, you'll need systematic approaches to scale learning across teams and departments. This means creating structured programs while maintaining the flexibility to support different learning needs.

Cross-team Forums

Regular meetings where different teams can share what they're learning about using AI. The Gen AI Lead typically organizes these sessions, while Gen AI Champions often present their teams' experiences. I've seen these work really well when they're structured as monthly sessions where teams can present their successes, discuss challenges, and brainstorm solutions together. The Gen AI Lead or a Champion usually facilitates, making sure to capture key learnings that can be shared more widely. It's also a great way for the Gen AI Lead to spot patterns and identify which approaches are working best across different parts of the organization.

As your champions develop deeper expertise, especially in agent implementation, these forums can evolve to include dedicated sessions where champions share technical implementation knowledge and discuss approaches to common challenges. This creates a community of practice within your broader forums, allowing champions to support each other while still keeping the wider organization informed about progress and learnings.

Center of Excellence

Every company needs to develop expertise in using Gen AI, and establishing something like a Center of Excellence is a great way to ensure this happens.

It is typically led by the Gen AI Lead and includes several dedicated Gen AI Champions. This can be a dedicated team or an informal group that collects and shares best practices, and helps teams apply Gen AI effectively. The goal is to build your organization's Gen AI muscle.

They should focus on building internal capabilities rather than just relying on external experts. This means developing your own expertise in prompt engineering, good Gen AI use cases, and eventually also designing and deploying AI agents. External experts often help get it started, but the goal is to build self-sufficiency. Think of it as building a new core competency for your organization - one that will be crucial for staying competitive in the years ahead.

As your organization progresses to implementing AI agents, your Center of Excellence becomes even more valuable. It can serve as the hub for your champion community, developing shared standards and patterns for agent development, exploring new capabilities of agent platforms, and accelerating your organization's learning curve with agents. The collective expertise of your champions becomes a powerful asset as you scale your agent implementation efforts, and your Center of Excellence provides the structure to harness this expertise effectively.

✏️ Exercise: Launch Your Gen AI Learning Journey

Take your first steps towards kicking off Gen AI learning in your organization:

1. **Design Learning Mix** Create a simple learning plan showing:

   - Map current learning activities to build on
   - Add new learning activities to start with
   - Assign internal experts/champions

2. **Plan Implementation** Map out how to make it happen:

- Required resources and approvals
- Key stakeholders to involve
- Potential barriers and solutions
- Communication approach

3. **Create First Event** Plan your kickoff activity in detail:

- Choose format (lunch & learn, workshop, etc.)
- Create agenda and materials
- Identify and invite participants
- Set up practical arrangements

By the end of this exercise, you'll have a concrete plan for launching Gen AI learning in your organization, including a fully prepared first event. Even if you need approvals, having this ready will help you move forward quickly once you get them.

Bonus: If possible, run your first planned event within a week of completing this exercise - momentum matters!

From Learning to Strategy

Let me wrap up what we covered about driving learning in your organization. The central message is that learning needs evolve as you progress through different maturity levels. While some foundational activities support learning across all levels, specific capabilities become crucial at each stage of the journey.

Remember - this learning journey takes time. Don't expect everyone to become an AI expert overnight. However, if you create the right conditions and support the right capabilities at each level, you'll be amazed at how quickly people can adapt and start creating value with these new tools.

In the next chapter, we'll explore how to develop a comprehensive strategy that builds on this foundation of learning. With your organization actively building AI capabilities across different maturity levels, you're ready to think systematically about where and how to apply these new tools for maximum impact.

Driver 5: Strategy

After you've built momentum with learning and experimentation, it's time to develop a strategy for systematic Gen AI implementation. In this chapter, I'll share what I've learned about creating and executing effective Gen AI strategies that drive real organizational transformation.

💭 **Reflect: Your Gen AI Strategy**

Take a moment to consider these questions:

- What kind of organization do you want to become when you reach Level 4 maturity with Gen AI?
- How would you develop a strategy that moves you from your current level toward that vision?

Your answers will help frame your thinking as we explore how to create an effective Gen AI strategy.

Strategic Foundations

While your organization may currently be focused on Level 1 or 2 maturity - helping individuals and teams use Gen AI effectively - strategic planning requires looking further ahead to Levels 3 and 4. This is where the truly transformative potential of Gen AI emerges, as organizations move from basic tool usage to deploying custom AI agents and building integrated human-AI teams.

Let me walk you through how to move from early experiments to a real strategy for Gen AI. I've found that before diving into traditional strategy work, you need two important things in place.

First, you need some real learning and experimentation with Gen AI. This is where most organizations start, and it's exactly the right thing to do. You try things out, see what works, and build some confidence with the technology.

Then comes the really interesting part - thinking about what the future might look like. This is where you do some strategic foresight work and think through different scenarios for how Gen AI might develop. I'll cover this in more detail in the next section, but the core idea is to not just assume one future, but to think through different possibilities.

Once you have both practical experience and a good understanding of possible futures, then you can do the traditional strategy work effectively. This means setting a clear vision, identifying strategic priorities, planning concrete initiatives, and creating a compelling story - all of which we'll explore in detail.

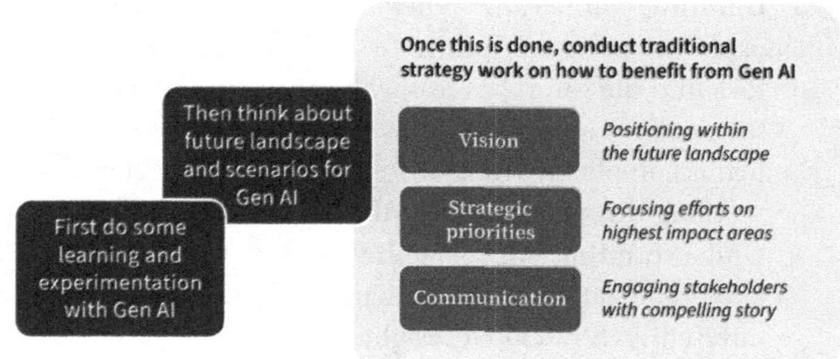

Figure 35. Setting strategy for Gen AI adoption

Strategic Foresight

When we work with organizations on Gen AI strategy, we often use strategic foresight to help them envision what Level 4 maturity might look like in their context. This structured approach helps teams think beyond their current level of Gen AI adoption to understand the full potential of human-AI collaboration.

Let me explain a bit what strategic foresight is and why it's so important when we think about Gen AI. Strategic foresight is about exploring and anticipating different possible futures, instead of just betting everything on a single hunch. It helps organizations deal with uncertainty by looking at different scenarios that might play out.

What makes this particularly valuable for Gen AI strategy isn't about deciding whether to pursue augmentation - I've tried to make a strong case for why this is the best path forward in almost all cases. Rather, strategic foresight helps you in three important ways:

1. **Building conviction**: When leaders actually spend time exploring potential futures firsthand - dipping their toes into the future, so to speak - their conviction about the need for action increases dramatically. I've seen teams completely transform their sense of urgency after working through different AI scenarios together.
2. **Understanding your specific context**: Every industry and organization will experience Gen AI's impact differently. Strategic foresight helps you identify which aspects matter most in your context and which capabilities will be most valuable for your specific situation.
3. **Clarifying timing decisions**: While we know Gen AI capabilities are advancing rapidly, foresight work helps you understand the sequence and pace that makes sense for your organization - what to focus on now versus later.

Exploring Key Dimensions

When we think about how Gen AI might develop, there are many dimensions we need to consider. Through our work with different organizations, I've seen some key dimensions that consistently shape how Gen AI will impact specific industries:

- How fast Gen AI capabilities advance
- Whether adoption focuses on automation or augmentation
- The level of new job creation vs displacement
- How much regulation affects Gen AI development and use

- Whether major AI players start moving into traditional industries
- How important proprietary data becomes
- The rate at which organizations adopt Gen AI
- How Gen AI affects robotics and physical automation
- The types of new services that emerge

Different dimensions matter more or less depending on your industry and context. For example, if you're in healthcare, regulation might be your most critical dimension. But if you're in retail, the connection between Gen AI and robotics might matter more.

Creating Scenarios

When we do strategic foresight, we start by looking at all the different ways things could play out. Through our work with organizations, we've found that certain patterns often emerge that help focus the conversation.

Looking at how different dimensions interact, we often see three types of scenarios emerge:

1. **Stagnation Scenarios**: The tech progress unexpectedly halts, strict regulations kick in, or organizations move too slowly or resist change. They make minimal investments in Gen AI capabilities and fail to build the learning culture needed for successful adoption. This leaves them vulnerable to disruption and talent loss.
2. **Automation-Only Scenarios**: Organizations implement AI primarily to replace human work. They focus on cost reduction rather than augmentation, missing opportunities to create new value. This approach often leads to workforce resistance and limits long-term competitive advantage.

3. **Augmentation Scenarios**: Organizations focus on building human-AI collaboration capabilities. They invest in learning, experiment with new service models, and develop unique combinations of human and AI capabilities. These scenarios offer the most potential for sustainable competitive advantage and growth.

While we've established that augmentation scenarios represent the preferred path forward, what's valuable is exploring what specific version of augmentation makes sense in your industry and organizational context. There isn't just one "augmentation future" - there are many variations depending on your specific circumstances.

Understanding Scenario Implications

The most valuable foresight work comes from deeply exploring different versions of augmentation scenarios for your specific industry, while understanding the risks that could push you toward less desirable futures.

For **Augmentation Scenarios**, the key is identifying what specific version makes sense in your context:

- What unique combination of human and AI capabilities will create the most value for your customers?
- Which processes benefit most from human-AI collaboration in your industry?
- What new services or business models become possible?
- What competitive advantages can you create through your specific approach to augmentation?

This exploration helps you develop a clear vision of your preferred future while understanding what you need to build to get there.

At the same time, it's important to understand the **Risk Scenarios** that could derail your progress:

Automation-Only Risk: If your organization focuses primarily on cost reduction rather than augmentation, you might see short-term efficiency gains but miss larger opportunities. This risk is particularly high in industries with significant cost pressures or where leadership lacks understanding of Gen AI's full potential. When facing pressure to focus solely on automation and cost-cutting, push back by demonstrating the much larger value creation possible through augmentation. Don't settle for just making existing processes cheaper - constantly look for ways to create new value and transform how work gets done. The real danger is creating an efficiency-focused culture that can't pivot to innovation, leaving you vulnerable to competitors who develop more sophisticated human-AI capabilities.

Stagnation Risk: Moving too slowly or cautiously creates different risks. Organizations that fail to build Gen AI capabilities quickly enough may find themselves unable to catch up as the technology rapidly advances. This risk is especially relevant in industries with high regulatory barriers or legacy cultural resistance to change. My most common advice here is: Don't take "no" for an answer. When faced with regulatory hurdles or compliance concerns, the question should never be "if" but "how". Keep pushing forward, finding creative ways to progress while staying compliant. The real danger is falling so far behind that catching up becomes prohibitively expensive or time-consuming.

Understanding these risks helps you identify early warning signs and develop mitigation strategies to stay on your preferred augmentation path.

Capability Evolution Timing

One dimension that really matters when thinking about Gen AI strategy is the timing of when specific AI capabilities will be unlocked. Right now, the models are excellent at writing, but there are still many things knowledge workers spend time on that the models aren't quite reliable at yet.

For example, current AI models aren't great at creating complex Excel financial models or iterating on good slide decks. They don't have strong spatial thinking and can't really draw 2D or 3D structures freehand. But over time, these capabilities will get unlocked, and when that happens, it will have huge implications for businesses.

Let me give you a concrete example. In financial controlling, right now the models aren't good enough to work with complicated financial modeling Excel files. This means there's still huge room for human involvement. For companies with big finance departments, this is a major cost center. For accounting firms and financial consultants, this is a big revenue source.

But what happens when AI models become really good at this? Companies with internal financial controlling departments might keep their employees but do much more sophisticated work. Meanwhile, consultants that provide financial controlling services will have a tough time selling their expertise unless they become more sophisticated and adaptive.

I'm seeing a similar dynamic with SaaS services. There's now a trend where companies look at their most expensive software-as-a-service solutions and ask, "How complicated would it be for us to just replicate this with AI-written code?" For many solutions, it's not that difficult anymore. This doesn't mean the end of SaaS, but it does mean SaaS companies face a new source of competition - internally developed solutions created by suddenly much more capable IT departments.

This balance between value creation and cost will shift as new AI capabilities come online. Over time, more organizations will be able to do things in-house that they previously outsourced. When you're developing your Gen AI strategy, think carefully about which capabilities matter most in your industry and how their timing might affect your competitive position.

Monitoring and Adapting

As you develop your strategy, you'll need to track how things are actually evolving. Setting up a simple monitoring framework helps you spot early signs of which scenario is becoming more likely, so you can adjust your approach accordingly.

Focus on tracking indicators like:

- Gen AI capability development in your industry
- Regulatory changes affecting your specific sector
- Customer expectations and adoption patterns
- Competitor approaches to Gen AI implementation
- Workforce skill development and adaptation
- New service models emerging in your space

Review these regularly (at least quarterly) to refine your understanding of how your industry's specific version of the augmentation scenario is taking shape, and to identify any warning signs that you might be drifting toward risk scenarios.

Strategic foresight helps you understand the landscape of possibilities while identifying the specific version of augmentation that makes the most sense for your organization. With this understanding, you're ready to define exactly how you want to show up in that future - which brings us to developing your vision for Gen AI.

Vision

Your Gen AI vision should paint a clear picture of what your organization will look like at Level 4 maturity, where humans and AI agents work together as unified teams. While you may currently be at an earlier level, having this North Star helps guide your transformation journey.

In Part 2, we explored the different types of AI agents that will emerge in Level 4 - from agents handling everyday tasks and managing information flows to those focused on customer value delivery.

Your vision needs to show how the addition of these different types of agents allows you to create new kinds of value that just weren't possible before. Maybe it's offering truly personalized services at a scale that was unimaginable. Or perhaps it's creating completely new products that combine AI capabilities with human insight in ways your competitors haven't thought of.

Let me share two mental models I use to help teams think about their vision. The first one looks at the demand side - what customers really value. Start by looking at the most premium offerings in your industry today. What makes people willing to pay top prices for these services? Then push it further - what would an even more premium offering look like?

For example, in financial services, premium clients get dedicated advisors who know their complete financial situation and proactively reach out with personalized guidance. With AI coworkers, you could extend this level of service to many more clients. Your advisors could manage relationships with 5x more clients while providing even deeper insights, because AI coworkers would continuously analyze market conditions, client portfolios, and potential opportunities. The human advisors would focus on understanding client goals, building trust, and providing judgment - while AI handles the analysis, monitoring, and preparation of recommendations.

The second model flips this around and looks at the supply side. Imagine you could suddenly add 10 or even 100 times more people to your organization, but these additional workers were essentially free. How would you change your services? What new offerings could you create?

Consider a customer support team. With 100x more capacity, you wouldn't just answer tickets faster - you'd completely reimagine your approach. You might monitor all customer interactions across every channel in real-time, proactively reaching out when you detect potential issues. You could create personalized help resources for each customer based on their specific product configuration and usage patterns. You might even assign dedicated support agents to every customer, regardless of tier. This is exactly the kind of transformation that's possible with AI coworkers - they let you massively scale up your capabilities without the usual cost constraints.

Using both these models helps you think bigger about what's possible. The demand side shows you what people truly value, while the supply side reveals how AI can help you deliver that value in completely new ways.

What makes a vision really powerful is when it connects

directly to your organization's deeper purpose. When you link Gen AI capabilities to why your organization exists in the first place, the transformation becomes much more meaningful. For example, if you're a healthcare provider whose purpose is improving patient outcomes, your vision might show how AI coworkers help clinicians spend less time on documentation and more time with patients, while also catching potential issues earlier through continuous monitoring. Or if you're an educational institution, your vision might show how AI tutors give every student personalized support while letting teachers focus on building motivation, creativity, and critical thinking. Connecting to purpose helps people see Gen AI not just as a productivity tool, but as a way to fulfill your organization's most important goals.

Developing this vision works best as a collaborative process involving both leadership and teams from across the organization. We try to bring together a diverse group including:

- Senior leaders who understand the strategic direction
- Customer-facing teams who know what clients truly value
- Operational teams who understand current processes and limitations
- People who have already started experimenting with Gen AI

Together, this group explores both mental models, shares their perspectives on what's possible, and crafts a vision that's both ambitious and authentic to the organization. Having diverse input not only creates a stronger vision but also builds early buy-in from key stakeholders.

You need to paint a picture that's both ambitious and concrete. Show how these different types of agents, working together with your people, will help you compete in a market where Gen AI has transformed what's possible. Your vision document should be detailed enough - a couple of pages at least - to give people a real sense of what you're aiming for.

Once you have a clear vision like this, you need a way to track progress towards it. That's where our measurement framework comes in, which I'll explain next.

✏️ Exercise: Develop Your Strategic Foresight and Gen AI Vision

This exercise helps you explore possible futures and create a compelling vision for your organization's Gen AI journey.

1. **Explore Key Dimensions** (30 minutes)

   - List the 4-5 most critical dimensions affecting Gen AI in your industry
   - Rate each dimension on uncertainty (low/medium/high) and potential impact
   - Identify which combinations would create your preferred augmentation scenario

2. **Sketch Your Augmentation Future** (45 minutes)

   - Describe your preferred version of an augmentation future:

- Which processes benefit most from human-AI collaboration?
- What unique value could you create for customers?
- How would work be organized differently?

- Identify 2-3 risk scenarios that could derail your progress
- List early warning signs to watch for

3. **Create Your Gen AI Vision** (45 minutes)

- Apply both mental models to your organization:

  - Demand-side: What would your "premium" service look like with AI?
  - Supply-side: What could you do with 10x or 100x more capability?

- Draft a 1-2 page vision document that includes:

  - The future state of work in your organization
  - How different types of AI agents will transform key processes
  - Specific new value you'll create for customers
  - Connection to your organization's deeper purpose

This exercise helps you move from abstract possibilities to a concrete vision that can guide your Gen AI transformation journey.

Strategic Priorities

After developing your vision for Level 4 maturity, the next step is figuring out where to focus your efforts. While basic tool adoption (Level 1) and team-level process improvements (Level 2) create important foundations, your strategic priorities should focus primarily on the transformative opportunities that emerge at Levels 3 and 4 - where custom AI agents and human-AI teams can create breakthrough value.

What works best is breaking this down into three main parts. First, we need to understand the total value that Gen AI could create for your organization. Then we do a systematic diagnostic to find specific opportunities. Finally, we turn the best opportunities into concrete initiatives that we can actually execute.

What's really important here is to be systematic but practical - we want to find opportunities that can drive significant impact.

Total Value at Stake

The total value Gen AI can create for your organization depends on what kind of vision you're working towards.

If your vision is mostly about making existing work more efficient at Levels 1 and 2, you'll see one level of value. Even basic AI chatbots are delivering 15-30% productivity gains through faster writing, analysis, and routine tasks. But if your vision is more transformative - reaching Levels 3 and 4 with AI agents handling entire workflows or creating completely new ways of working - then the value potential is much bigger. Organizations that systematically implement Gen AI across workflows and processes, using AI agents as true coworkers, can see 3-5x productivity improvements.

When we talk about productivity improvements, what we mean is that people can do their work faster. This creates time that we can use in different ways. We could cut costs by reducing headcount. Or we could use that time to create new value, which is better but requires some level of innovation. The risk, of course, is that the time just gets eaten up by more meetings and bureaucracy. But in companies that are good at innovation, most of that freed-up time goes into new, valuable work.

So how do you figure out the total value at stake from Gen AI for your organization? Start by looking at your main areas of work. Think about how they would work with really capable AI coworkers helping out. Don't get stuck trying to calculate exact numbers - a rough estimate is fine. What you need is a business case that shows big enough numbers to get your management team excited, while still being believable.

Opportunity Diagnostic

With a sense of the total value at stake, the next step is finding specific opportunities to capture that value. This needs a systematic diagnostic approach.

Start by breaking down the total opportunity by major areas

of your organization - like HR, Marketing, Customer Support, and other key functions. This helps you understand where the biggest potential lies and gives clear ownership for capturing value in each area.

Then, for each major area, assess:

- Potential value: Time saved, quality improved, new capabilities
- Technical feasibility: How readily Gen AI solutions could help
- Organizational readiness: Teams' ability to adopt new ways of working
- Speed to impact: How quickly you could see results

Don't try to analyze everything in detail at once. Do a quick first pass to identify promising areas, then drill down only where it makes sense. Focus your detailed analysis on opportunities that combine high potential value with clear feasibility and quick wins.

At the end of this exercise, you should have a clear map showing the value potential for each major area of your organization. For example, you might find that customer service has a 40% productivity opportunity worth $2M annually, while sales has a 25% opportunity worth $1.5M. This kind of breakdown helps you assign clear ownership and targets to different leaders across the organization. Having these numbers, even if they're rough estimates, makes it much easier to track progress and hold people accountable as you move forward with implementation.

🌍 Real World Example: Documenting Use Cases Across the Value Spectrum

A customer of ours, a global industrial company facing the challenge of managing hundreds of emerging Gen AI use cases developed a simple but effective categorization approach.

They created a two-track system that distinguished between small improvements that teams could implement themselves versus larger initiatives requiring formal project structures. For the smaller improvements, they built a searchable prompt library where teams could share effective prompts for common tasks.

For larger opportunities, they developed a more structured database tracking potential business impact, required resources, and implementation status. This allowed him to identify which high-value use cases to prioritize for formal development while still encouraging the organic spread of smaller improvements.

One particularly high-value use case they identified involved using Gen AI to analyze complex contract documentation from customer projects and automatically distribute the relevant information to appropriate departments – a process that had previously required days of manual work by specialized staff.

🌍 Real World Example: Three-Tier Strategic Framework

Another customer of ours, also an industrial company, developed a three-tiered strategic framework for Gen AI adoption that helped them balance immediate productivity gains with longer-term business transformation.

Their lowest tier focused on personal productivity – ensuring all knowledge workers had access to Gen AI tools and the skills to use them effectively. This created immediate value while building overall AI literacy across the organization.

The middle tier concentrated on developing specialized Gen AI solutions for specific business processes, with formal evaluation criteria to decide which opportunities warranted investment and whether to build or buy solutions.

The highest tier explored how Gen AI might fundamentally transform their business model and organizational structure, with executive programs designed to help leadership envision possible futures and identify new revenue opportunities.

"This tiered approach helped us maintain momentum," their Gen AI Lead explained. "The personal productivity level delivered immediate wins that built excitement, while the higher tiers ensured we weren't just making existing processes more efficient but were also preparing for more fundamental transformation."

By structuring their strategy this way, they ensured both short-term wins to maintain enthusiasm and long-term thinking to prepare for industry disruption.

Strategic Initiatives

Once you've identified and prioritized opportunities, you need to turn them into concrete initiatives. Break larger opportunities into smaller, manageable pieces. And of course, use Gen AI to help you describe the initiatives. Good initiatives need:

- Clear value targets linked to your diagnostic
- Specific scope and timeline
- Dedicated ownership and resources
- Defined success criteria

Start with initiatives that build momentum while working toward bigger transformational goals. The goal isn't to plan everything perfectly from the start. It's to create a clear first set of initiatives that will help your organization start moving in the right direction. We'll talk more about how to actually drive and coordinate these initiatives when we get to scaling.

Communication

When I work with organizations on Gen AI transformation, I use the same story about urgency that I shared in Chapter

2. Remember how we talked about building that sense of urgency? It starts by pointing out that even the simplest AI chatbots are already delivering real value. Some analysts estimate about a 30% productivity boost just from the chatbots available today. Then I help people see how we're moving from these basic chatbots to much more capable AI coworkers that can handle entire workflows independently. If we look ahead, it's not hard to imagine organizations filled with these AI coworkers, making us many times more productive than we are now.

But here's the thing: this is about more than just productivity. It's about linking the transformation to why your organization exists in the first place. When we talk with teams about Gen AI, we find that focusing only on efficiency or cost savings doesn't really inspire people. But when we connect it to their deeper purpose - to what the organization is really trying to achieve - that's when people get excited. We talk about how AI coworkers can take over the routine tasks that keep people from doing their most meaningful work. This lets them spend more time on the parts of their job that really matter, the things that drew them to this work in the first place. That's the story that really grabs people — Gen AI as a way to help them do more of what they care about most.

I also love using this analogy of centaurs, where the half human, half horse centaur symbolizes how we can work side-by-side with AI. Our human strengths blend with AI's processing power, giving everyone "superpowers". When AI handles the repetitive, low-impact tasks, our people have more time and energy to focus on our higher purpose. And they can do this work at a completely different level than before. Including this in the communication about why your organization needs to adopt Gen AI makes it much more exciting - it's not just about being more efficient, it's about having a bigger impact on the things we care about most.

The other important point is that this isn't a quick fix. It's a learning journey. People need time and practice to understand how AI tools can fit into their workflows. But that's part of what makes it exciting. Once they do, they start discovering new ways of working and solving problems that just weren't possible before. Even small everyday tasks get a bit easier, leaving more space for creativity or critical thinking.

Putting all this together, I usually frame the story like this: "We have a deeper purpose – whatever it is that drives our organization. We're at the beginning of a major shift that can help us achieve that purpose in fresh ways. As we learn to partner with AI coworkers, every single person here can level up their abilities. We need to start now because this technology moves quickly, and organizations that learn fast will have a real edge in fulfilling their mission.

When you anchor every new initiative – like giving people access to AI tools or launching training programs – into that broader vision, people see why it matters. It's not "another IT thing". It's a crucial step toward the future where human potential is amplified towards fulfilling our shared purpose.

I've seen many organizations get bogged down in handling all the mundane details of implementation - things like access controls, usage policies, and tool configurations. When this happens, they often lose sight of the compelling "why" behind their Gen AI transformation (in the sense that Simon Sinek talks about). So it's really worth getting this story right at the start, and then consistently bringing people back to it. Don't let your teams get stuck only thinking about the "what" - keep reminding them of the "why".

Of course, this story works best when it's authentic. You'll want to shape it around your organization's unique purpose and culture. If you do that well, you'll have a powerful narrative that keeps everyone motivated through the ups and downs of this transformation journey.

When communicating your Gen AI strategy, help people understand how different initiatives connect to advancing through maturity levels. Show how foundational work at Levels 1-2 creates capabilities needed for more transformative Level 3-4 initiatives. This helps people see both the immediate value of current efforts and the bigger transformation ahead.

🌍 Real World Example: Balancing Internal Adoption and External Advocacy

A customer of ours, a labor union, faced a unique scaling challenge - balancing their internal Gen AI adoption with their responsibility to represent their members' interests in how AI was being implemented in their industry.

"As a union, we needed to both embrace AI internally and ensure our members' interests were protected as their employers began implementing the same technologies," their digital transformation leader explained. "This created an interesting dynamic in how we approached our own adoption."

They resolved this by establishing two parallel workstreams:

- An internal team focused on implementing Gen AI tools to improve their own operations

- A policy team dedicated to developing positions on responsible AI implementation in their members' workplaces

The internal team's experiences directly informed the policy team's work, giving them practical insights into both the benefits and potential issues their members might face. Meanwhile, their policy positions helped shape their own internal guidelines.

"Our dual role actually became an advantage," their Gen AI Lead noted. "We could demonstrate responsible adoption internally while advocating for the same standards externally. This stance - that AI should augment rather than replace workers - became central to both our internal messaging and external advocacy."

✏️ Exercise: Create Your Gen AI Strategic Roadmap

This exercise helps you translate your vision into practical action through strategic priorities and compelling communication.

1. **Value Mapping** (30 minutes)

   - Estimate the total Gen AI value opportunity

for your organization

- Break down this value by business function/area
- For 2-3 high-potential areas, assess:

  - Potential value (productivity gains, new capabilities)
  - Technical feasibility
  - Organizational readiness
  - Speed to impact

2. **Initiative Planning** (40 minutes)

   - Create 3-4 strategic initiatives:

     - 1-2 foundational initiatives (tools, training, access)
     - 1-2 impact initiatives (process redesign, agents)

   - For each initiative, define:

     - Clear value targets and success metrics
     - Specific scope and timeline
     - Required resources and ownership

3. **Develop Your Narrative** (30 minutes)

   - Draft your transformation story:

- Why this matters for your organization now
- How it connects to your broader purpose
- What success will look like at each stage

- Create a 2-minute pitch and a longer narrative version
- Identify key metaphors or examples that resonate in your context

4. **Communication Planning** (20 minutes)

- Map out how to share this story across your organization:

  - Key audiences and what matters most to each
  - Communication channels and formats
  - Frequency and reinforcement approach

This exercise helps you move from vision to action by creating concrete initiatives and a compelling story that drives momentum for your Gen AI transformation.

From Strategy to Scale

As you develop your Gen AI strategy, remember that progress through maturity levels isn't automatic - it requires deliberate effort and investment. Your strategy needs to balance building strong foundations at early levels while pushing toward the transformative potential of Levels 3 and 4.

In the next chapter, we'll explore how to take your strategy from paper to practice - scaling Gen AI adoption across your organization. With a solid strategic foundation in place, you're ready to start spreading successful practices and building momentum for broader transformation.

Driver 6: Scale

In the last chapter, I talked about how to develop your Gen AI strategy. Now comes the really interesting part - taking all that learning and strategic thinking and scaling it across your organization.

💭 **Reflect: Scaling Gen AI in Your Organization**
Take a moment to consider these questions:

- What are the biggest barriers to widespread Gen AI adoption in your organization?
- How can you help successful Gen AI practices spread across your organization?

Your answers will help you identify your most important challenges as we explore the different aspects of scaling Gen AI adoption.

The Three Pillars of Scaling Gen AI

As we have worked with organizations on scaling their Gen AI adoption, we've seen some patterns emerge. We've seen three elements that need to work together.

1. Strategic Orchestration - Track progress on key metrics and coordinate initiatives across teams
2. Innovation Empowerment - Support teams' own AI projects and help spread successful examples
3. Change Enablement - Help people learn, remove obstacles, and address concerns early

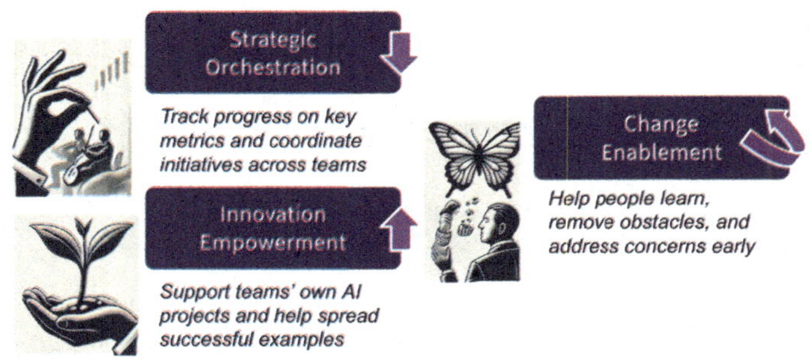

Figure 36. Three Pillars of Scaling

We have courses for Gen AI Leads. When we come to the part where we talk about scaling Gen AI, the participants are often quite aware and feel equipped for the first pillar, while they have not thought as much about the second and third pillar.

Because of this, I'll keep the first pillar rather light, putting more emphasis on the others.

Strategic Orchestration

Remember how we talked about developing your Gen AI strategy? Now it's time to put that into action across your organization. As you scale up through different maturity levels, your orchestration needs evolve significantly. At Level 1, you're coordinating widespread tool adoption and tracking basic usage metrics. By Level 2, you're managing team-level process transformations and measuring their impact. At Level 3, you're orchestrating more complex agent development projects with deeper ROI metrics. Your PMO approach has to adapt to these changing needs while maintaining consistent oversight.

I've found that successful scaling requires two key elements working together. First, you need a structured way to coordinate and drive initiatives across teams. Second, you need clear metrics to track both progress and impact. Let me explain how to set up both.

Program Management Office

In my experience, it's really helpful to set up a PMO (Program Management Office) for your Gen AI initiatives. Many companies already have a Program Management Office to track and coordinate their strategic initiatives. If that's the case, the Gen AI initiatives could be linked to that. It doesn't need to be complicated - it's just a structured way to follow up on all the different projects happening across your organization. As a Gen AI lead, this is one of your key tools for success.

You need to:

- Keep track of what's happening where
- Make sure resources are going to the right places
- Help teams learn from each other
- Spot and support emerging opportunities
- Link project results to strategic goals

And, maybe this goes without saying, since by this point you as a Gen AI Lead are of course up to speed with using Gen AI tools, but they can help you save a lot of time here.

Measurement Framework

When it comes to measuring Gen AI impact, I've found it helpful to think about metrics along two dimensions. First, how quickly we'll see results - from leading indicators that show progress immediately to lagging indicators that demonstrate real impact over time. Second, how soon we can define the metrics in detail - some we can start tracking right away, while others need more learning and experimentation before we can articulate them clearly. Let's look at three types of metrics that develop over time.

Process Metrics

These are your leading indicators - metrics you can start tracking right away to show how your Gen AI adoption is progressing:

- **Tool usage**: Track how frequently and extensively people use Gen AI tools, including number of active users, session frequency, and feature adoption. This gives you immediate visibility into adoption rates and helps identify both power users and areas needing more support.
- **Self-reported value**: Run a simple monthly pulse survey asking "On a scale of 1-10, how useful is Gen AI in your daily work?" If you can move that average from 2 to 8, you can be quite confident that real impact will follow.

- **Prompt use cases**: Count individual productivity improvements where someone has created a simple prompt template that they can use in their daily work. This shows how people are starting to integrate Gen AI into their personal workflows.
- **Team use cases**: Track team-level workflow changes where a group has coherently redesigned how they work together using Gen AI tools. These represent deeper integration of Gen AI into business processes.
- **Impact use cases**: Monitor opportunities where you can quantify the business impact through a clear business case and that typically require budget to pursue. These often involve developing specialized AI agents and represent your highest-value transformation opportunities.

Operational Metrics

These show up in the middle term and demonstrate real changes in how work gets done, you probably have to think a bit to nail down exactly which metrics are most relevant for you to measure. Here are some examples:

- **Aspects of NPS**: Look at specific elements of your Customer Net Promoter Score that Gen AI initiatives should influence, such as response speed, solution quality, and customer satisfaction.
- **Aspects of eNPS**: Monitor employee satisfaction metrics related to tool effectiveness, particularly questions about whether Gen AI helps people do their best work and increases job satisfaction.
- **Quality metrics**: Track specific quality indicators relevant to your business, such as error rates, accuracy

levels, and consistency measures across different processes.

- **Lead times**: Measure how Gen AI impacts the speed of central business processes, from customer response times to internal workflow completion rates.

Financial Metrics

When it comes to financial metrics, you need to develop them step by step. Remember in Chapter 4 when we talked about the total value at stake from Gen AI? That's where you start - with that big, bold vision of what's possible when you fully embrace AI agents as coworkers. We saw that organizations systematically implementing Gen AI could see 3-5x productivity improvements.

That total impact goal becomes your North Star, but to make it real, you need to break it down:

- **Total impact goal**: Set clear targets for overall productivity improvements expected from Gen AI initiatives across the organization. This should align with the value at stake analysis from your strategy work. When teams save time through Gen AI, we can either capture this as cost savings through reduced headcount, or create new value by using that time for more productive work - but this needs clear plans to ensure the time doesn't just get absorbed into existing activities.
- **Impact breakdown by function/area**: Once you have confidence in your total goal, break it down by department and function. This lets you delegate clear targets to different leaders - for example, telling your customer service director they need to deliver 30% of the total productivity gains.

- **Realized impact by initiative**: As managers work to hit their targets, they'll naturally want ways to prove their progress. This is where those impact use cases we tracked in our process metrics become crucial - they feed directly into measuring realized financial impact. Each successful use case helps build toward the area's overall target.

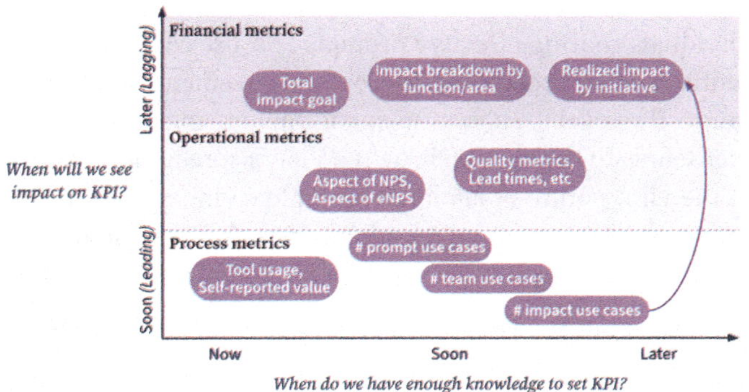

Figure 37. Evolution of GenAI metrics

This progression creates a powerful link between your process metrics and financial results. When managers see they need to deliver specific financial targets, they become hungry for more impact use cases, creating natural pull for innovation and adoption.

You'll get the most momentum if you work on all three types in parallel. The process metrics help you prove progress quickly, the operational metrics show you're making real impact, and the financial metrics keep you focused on the big picture. But here's what's really important - start measuring your process metrics right now, even if you're just getting started with Gen AI. Having this baseline data will be incredibly valuable as you move forward.

Innovation Empowerment

There's something really special about Gen AI that sets it apart from other technology transformations I've seen. This natural spread of innovation happens differently at each maturity level, but follows similar patterns. At Level 1, it's individuals sharing effective prompts and use cases. At Level 2, entire teams spread their process improvements to other groups. By Level 3, successful agent implementations inspire other teams to develop their own. What's spreading changes, but the viral nature of adoption - people trying something, getting excited, and showing others - remains consistent across levels.

I've found that this viral spread isn't just happening with consumers. It's happening inside organizations too. When people discover how Gen AI can help them work better, they naturally want to share it with their colleagues. This creates an amazing opportunity for scaling Gen AI adoption across your organization.

So while having a structured PMO approach is important, I've seen that the most powerful scaling happens when you tap into this natural enthusiasm. The wildfire method we talked about earlier - creating the right conditions for Gen AI to spread organically through your organization, just like a wildfire spreads through a forest - is even more relevant here than it was for Agile transformations.

When you're scaling Gen AI adoption, I've found that it's really important to be flexible about where you focus your efforts. Sometimes the teams that look perfect on paper aren't the ones that will drive the most impact. Instead, I've learned to look for teams that are genuinely excited about Gen AI and already starting to experiment with it. These teams often move faster and achieve better results than teams that are just following a top-down directive. So while your strategy might point you in one direction, don't be afraid to shift your priorities based on where you see real enthusiasm and momentum building.

I remember working with one Gen AI lead who had planned for their marketing team to lead their Gen AI initiatives. On paper, it made perfect sense - they had a perfect use case that aligned with their strategic priorities. But she noticed that the after-sales team was more excited about Gen AI. They were already experimenting with it and coming up with creative ideas. Even though they weren't the "obvious" choice, their enthusiasm and proactivity made them perfect for leading the charge.

Figure 38. The Wildfire Method

To support the Gen AI Champions and help spread the fire,

you need to do a few key things. First, remove unnecessary bureaucracy that might slow them down. Create safe spaces where teams can experiment with Gen AI without fear of failure. When teams try something new, celebrate both their successes and their "good failures" - the ones where they learned something valuable. And make sure to provide technical support when teams need it.

But the real magic happens when you help these success stories spread. Create forums where teams can share what they've learned. Help connect teams who are working on similar challenges. When someone finds a great way to use Gen AI, make sure other teams hear about it. And always link these successes back to your organization's bigger goals, so people can see how their Gen AI experiments are contributing to something larger.

This combination - supporting the Gen AI Champions and helping spread their successes - creates a powerful flywheel effect. Each success story inspires more teams to try Gen AI, leading to more successes, which inspires even more teams. It's like adding fuel to the fire, but in a good way. And before you know it, you've got Gen AI adoption spreading faster than any top-down rollout could achieve.

Change Enablement

When I work with organizations on scaling Gen AI, I often see them focus mostly on the technical and process parts. But there's something really important that often gets missed - helping people through this change. The support needed evolves significantly across maturity levels. At Level 1, it's about building confidence with basic tools. Level 2 requires helping entire teams reimagine their processes. By Level 3, we're supporting people in working with autonomous agents - a much bigger psychological shift. The principles of change enablement stay constant, but how we apply them must adapt to these different challenges.

Keeping the Inspiring Story Alive

Remember us covering communication in the Strategy chapter? Keep talking about how Gen AI helps your organization achieve its purpose, about how AI coworkers can handle routine tasks and give your people superpowers. People need to hear the story multiple times, in different ways, to really connect with it. But now, as you're scaling, you can add real examples from your own organization - stories of teams who are already seeing these benefits.

Supporting the Learning Journey at Scale

Earlier in Learning chapter, we dove into learning approaches that work. All activities become even more important as you scale up. But now you need to think about how to make them work across the whole organization.

I've found that it works best to keep running the same kinds of activities we talked about before - the training sessions, coaching, peer mentoring, and hands-on projects. But now you need to be more systematic about it. You need to make sure these learning opportunities are available to everyone, not just the early adopters.

The key is to keep that learning momentum going. Don't think "we did the training, now we're done." Instead, think about how to make learning a natural part of how people work with Gen AI every day.

Creating Psychological Safety

Here's something really important that I've learned - when you're scaling Gen AI adoption, you need to create an environment where people feel safe to learn and experiment. This means a few key things:

First, be really open about the changes that Gen AI will bring. Yes, it will make some work more efficient. Yes, some roles might change. Don't shy away from these conversations. Instead, be clear about your plans to help people evolve in their roles or find new opportunities.

Second, make it okay for people to speak up about their concerns. When someone worries about being replaced by AI, don't dismiss it. Listen and address it directly. Show them how you're planning to help them grow and adapt.

Third, support people who are trying new things with Gen AI. When someone experiments and it doesn't work out perfectly, treat it as a learning opportunity, not a failure. This helps build the confidence people need to really embrace these new ways of working.

Looking at Behaviors and Consequences

When we want to create change in organizations, what we really want is results. And results come from behaviors - the actual things people do differently. To help think about this more clearly, there's a really useful framework called Organizational Behavior Management (OBM), and that I've found helpful when scaling Gen AI adoption.

The OBM framework looks at three parts of any change:

- Activation (or Antecedent) - everything that happens before the behavior we want

- Behavior - the actual actions people take
- Consequences - what happens after the behavior

In any transformation, the common pattern is that organizations often focus about 90% of their effort on activation. They set goals, make plans, communicate, launch initiatives, and run training programs. But they don't pay enough attention to consequences - the things that happen after people try these new behaviors. This is exactly backwards from what research shows works best, as we should focus 90% on the consequences.

Let me give you an example. Let's say a customer service team decides to redesign their ticket handling process using Gen AI. The activation might include communication about adopting Gen AI, some basic Gen AI training sessions. The behavior is the team actually deciding to try to do process re-engineering and implementing their new workflow with Gen AI. And the consequences? Well, there are the direct ones - they handle tickets faster, spend less time on repetitive responses, and get to focus on more interesting customer problems. But what is probably even more important are the organizational consequences - did their manager publicly recognized their initiative? Did IT fast-track their tool requests? Did the Gen AI Lead help them overcome bureaucratic hurdles? Did other teams hear about their success and get inspired? These organizational consequences often determine whether the change sticks and spreads.

As a Gen AI Lead, you need to think carefully about these types of consequences. What happens when people show the behaviors you want to see? For example, if you want people to experiment with using Gen AI in their work, what happens when they do? Do they get recognition? Does it help their career? Or does it just mean more work for them?

I've found that unless you make sure there are positive consequences for the behaviors you want, the change won't stick. This means:

- Recognizing and celebrating when people use Gen AI in innovative ways
- Making Gen AI skills part of how you evaluate and develop people
- Ensuring that using Gen AI tools actually makes people's work easier or more interesting
- Supporting teams that take initiative to transform their workflows with Gen AI

🌍 Real World Example: Creating Positive Consequences for AI Adoption

A customer of ours, a major manufacturing company, leveraged their existing continuous improvement program to accelerate Gen AI adoption.

For years, they had run a "3i" program where each employee was expected to implement three improvements annually, with teams receiving bonuses when they met their targets. Each year featured a "focus area" where improvements received double credit. Recognizing the opportunity, they designated Gen AI as the focus area for the upcoming year.

This approach created immediate positive consequences for experimenting with Gen AI. Employees who developed effective prompts or AI-enabled workflows now received formal recognition and rewards. What began as scattered experiments quickly became a company-wide movement as teams competed to develop the most impactful AI use cases.

"By connecting AI adoption to our existing improvement culture and reward systems, we created an environment where experimenting with AI was not just permitted but actively celebrated," their Gen AI Lead explained.

Bringing It All Together

Part of your role as a Gen AI Lead is to bring all these pieces together - communicating the story, continuous learning opportunities, psychological safety, and the right consequences for desired behaviors. When you get this right, you create an environment where Gen AI adoption can really flourish across your organization.

✏️ Exercise: Get Your Gen AI Scaling Flywheel Going

Once you've got some initial Gen AI initiatives running and seeing results, it's time to analyze what's working and create momentum for broader adoption. Here's how to take stock and accelerate your scaling efforts through three focused steps:

1. **Success Story Analysis** (45 min) Find and analyze 2-3 existing Gen AI success stories in your organization:

- For each success story:

    - What specifically made it work?
    - Which teams/people were involved?
    - What positive consequences followed?
    - How did word spread about it?

- Looking across stories:

    - What common patterns emerge?
    - Where are the natural enthusiasts?
    - What barriers did they overcome?

2. **Scaling Conditions** (45 min) Based on your analysis, outline how to create the right conditions for scaling:

- **Strategic Orchestration**:

    - Which 2-3 metrics matter most?
    - How will you track progress?
    - What governance is needed?

- **Innovation Empowerment**:

    - How to identify and support enthusiastic teams?
    - What forums for sharing success?

- Which bureaucratic barriers to remove?

- **Change Enablement**:

    - How to make learning continuously available?
    - What positive consequences to reinforce?
    - How to address common concerns?

3. **Next Actions** (30 min) Create a concrete 30-day action plan:

    - List 3 immediate actions for each pillar
    - Identify key people to involve
    - Schedule your first coordination meeting
    - Plan your first success-sharing event

This exercise helps you create practical plans for scaling Gen AI adoption that balance structured coordination with organic growth. Focus on specific, achievable actions that create the right conditions for success to spread.

Bonus: Find one team that's already enthusiastic about Gen AI and schedule a session to learn about their experience and how to help them succeed.

From Present to Future

Scaling Gen AI adoption is definitely a journey, and it's different from other technology transformations we've seen before. The key is finding the right balance between top-down direction and bottom-up innovation, while really focusing on helping people adapt to these new ways of working.

Success comes from combining structured coordination with organic growth - tracking progress systematically while supporting the natural enthusiasm that emerges when people discover how AI can help them work better. When you get this balance right, you create the conditions for lasting transformation.

In the epilogue, we'll look at what's coming next - the evolution from AI chatbots to true AI agents, and how organizations are starting to build hybrid teams where humans and AI work together as unified teams. But first, take a moment to reflect on how far we've come in understanding how to make Gen AI transformation work in practice.

Epilogue

As I put the finishing touches on this book, I can't help but reflect on how much has changed since I started writing it. I started my Gen AI journey when ChatGPT launched in late 2022. Like many others, I was amazed by what it could do. But what really got me excited was seeing how it could help organizations work in completely new ways. Since then, I've been on an incredible learning journey, working with many different organizations to help them adopt Gen AI.

I've made a choice with releasing a version of this book early. Like Carl-Henric Svanberg with Sweden's AI Commission report, I've decided to release it earlier than initially planned. The field is moving incredibly fast, and organizations need practical guidance now, not in six months. Sure, I could keep writing and refining for several more months - there's so much to cover, many concrete examples not included, and I'm learning new things every day. But I see too many organizations struggling with their Gen AI adoption right now. The frameworks and approaches in this book can help them move forward, and that's more important than having a perfectly polished manuscript.

Throughout this book, we've explored how adopting Gen AI and agents is different from other technology transformations. It's not about implementing complex technical systems - it's about helping people learn to work with AI in new ways. We've looked at how organizations can move from individual experimentation to having true human-AI teams. We've explored why augmenting people is more powerful than pure automation, and how teams can build key capabilities from prompt engineering to implementing agents. And we've examined how to orchestrate this transformation across the organization while enabling teams to drive adoption forward.

Looking ahead, I see two major developments that will shape how organizations work with Gen AI. And to be honest, by the time you read this, these developments might already be here - that's how fast things are moving.

First, and this one we've already covered quite a bit - we're moving rapidly from AI chatbots to true AI coworkers. These agents won't just respond to queries - they'll be able to handle entire workflows independently. They'll coordinate with each other, manage information flows, and multiply human capabilities in ways we're just beginning to understand.

Second, as a consequence of the first, we'll see the emergence of hybrid organizations where humans and AI agents work together as unified teams. This isn't just about automating tasks - it's about fundamentally rethinking how work gets done. We're learning that the most powerful approach is neither human-only nor AI-only, but rather human-AI collaboration where each brings their unique strengths.

At Ymnig AI, we're already working on these next frontiers. We help individuals and organizations adopt Gen AI and agents through our courses, coaching, and workshops. We work with everyone from board members thinking about strategy to Gen AI Leads driving transformation, and teams figuring out how to work with Gen AI in their daily work. We're learning new things every day by teaching, experimenting, and seeing what works in practice.

Beyond this, we provide a platform for AI agents and are especially excited about helping organizations bring these new capabilities to their teams. What we've found most effective is a connected journey where we first help build foundational capabilities through training, then empower champions to identify agent opportunities, and finally support them in implementing agents using our platform. This integrated approach ensures that technical implementation is always guided by clear business value and organizational readiness.

We're seeing firsthand how organizations adapt their ways of working as AI agents become part of their teams. We are growing fast and see way more opportunities than we can grasp. If you're interested in being part of our journey - as a customer, partner, or employee - please don't hesitate to reach out.

We're just at the beginning of this journey. The capabilities of AI systems are advancing incredibly quickly, and we're constantly discovering new ways they can help organizations work better.

I believe that organizations that learn to work effectively with AI coworkers will have an enormous advantage in the years ahead. But getting there takes time - it requires building new capabilities, rethinking processes, and helping people adapt to new ways of working.

That's why I wanted to share what I've learned so far, even though I know some of it might be outdated by the time you read this. The core principles and frameworks in this book will help you navigate your own Gen AI transformation journey. And I look forward to learning together as we continue exploring this incredible technology that's reshaping how we work.

The next chapter in this story is already being written. I'm excited to see what you'll help create.

Acknowledgements

Behind every book lies not just ideas and expertise, but a network of support that makes the work possible. This one is no exception.

First and foremost I want to thank Evelina, the love of my life. Her support created the space I needed to write this book amidst our beautifully chaotic life with three small children. Her patience, encouragement, and belief in this project sustained me through late nights and busy weekends. Without her partnership, these pages would simply not exist.

This book also represents the collective wisdom of many brilliant colleagues and collaborators who have shaped my understanding of Gen AI and its impact on how we work. Let me start by thanking my colleagues who have been instrumental in this journey.

Henrik Kniberg deserves special thanks, not just for writing the foreword, but for being my partner in exploring what Gen AI really means in practice. For more than a year now, we've worked closely together, grappling with and trying to understand what happens when these Gen AI models hit reality, co-exploring this space and pushing the frontier of practical knowledge.

Hans Brattberg gave me a piece of advice I took to heart: "If you want to learn something, host a course about it." His fearless approach to learning, holding courses, and writing books has been truly inspiring. At first, there was quite a bit of "fake it till you make it," but after running many workshops and courses, the faking part definitely decreased! This approach really accelerated my learning - both in preparing thoroughly for the workshops and courses and learning from all the discussions during them.

Åsa Martinsson deserves special thanks for combining sales leadership with masterful operational support. I could never have maintained the tempo of workshops and courses without her taking care of all the communication, process, and logistics, allowing me to concentrate solely on clients and content. The fact that we've been able to work with so many organizations in their Gen AI journey is in large part thanks to her work.

Getting feedback on a book is incredibly valuable - it helps clarify thinking, spot gaps, and make the content more useful for readers. I'm grateful to several colleagues who took the time to read early drafts and share their thoughts. Johan Sanderoth deserves extra credit for reading through the entire book multiple times and providing detailed input - his contributions were truly fantastic. Madelen Porserud and Erik Wenneborg also read through the book and gave valuable input that helped shape the final result.

I've been fortunate to work with over 60 companies on their Gen AI journeys. While I can't name them all for confidentiality reasons, I want to thank them for the trust they placed in me and for everything they taught me along the way. Each organization brought unique challenges and perspectives that helped shape my understanding of what happens when Gen AI meets the real world. I'd like to specifically thank Björn Rydberg, Susanne Blanke, Petter Brandt, Annie von Heijne, Sam Saatchi, Magnus Liungman, Jacob Stedman, Hanna Radtke Bergström, Peter Käll, and Teresa Tot, whose insights and collaboration have been particularly valuable. These are just a few of the many people whose discussions and feedback have been instrumental in shaping my thinking about Gen AI in practice.

I've had the privilege of training more than 1,000 people in Gen AI workshops and courses. Training is always a two-way street - I've learned as much from the participants as they hopefully learned from me. The discussions and questions during these sessions have been invaluable in deepening my understanding. I want to give special thanks to Ledarna, a Swedish labor union for managers, and particularly to Fredrik Gustafsson, Helene Weberyd, and Christina Werner for our most intense course collaboration. Together, we've conducted over 25 courses, as well as several webinars with hundreds of participants. This collaboration has been truly remarkable.

In terms of course collaborations, I've been fortunate to work with several exceptional individuals. Sanna Westerberg brought her deep expertise in change management to our first Gen AI Lead course. We embarked on a joint learning journey, combining her extensive experience in driving organizational change with understanding of Gen AI and what happens when organizations try to adopt it. Our collaboration helped shape my thinking about how to successfully drive change. I'm also grateful to Frida Mangen, Ted Solomon, and Line Thomson for our wonderful course collaborations, which have been invaluable learning experiences.

Staying current with the rapidly evolving field of Gen AI has been a challenge, with significant developments sometimes occurring multiple times in a single week. Philip at AI Explained has been a crucial source of understanding, helping me stay at the frontier of academic developments in Gen AI through his YouTube channel and Patreon account. I also want to thank Robert Wiblin and Luisa Rodriguez from the 80,000 Hours podcast, Dwarkesh Patel, and Lex Fridman for their thoughtful interviews with key figures in the AI world that have helped me understand the field's rapid development. Similarly, my discussions with Samuel Hägerstam have been invaluable for understanding the broader aspects of AI, including long-term horizon development, AI safety, and wider implications.

The book itself has benefited enormously from literary and structural input. Alexander Norén and Martin Kjellberg deserve special recognition for reading the manuscript and providing insights that helped transform it into something more compelling. While others helped ensure the content was accurate and useful, Alexander and Martin helped make the book a more engaging and well-structured piece of writing.

Finally, I want to thank Annelies Clauwaert for her exceptional design work. She transformed this manuscript into an actual book, creating the cover design and improving the illustrations throughout. Her visual expertise and attention to detail helped bring the concepts to life and made the book both more professional and more accessible. Thanks to her, the book not only conveys ideas but does so in a visually engaging way.

I've learned so much while writing this book - both from the writing itself and from all the people who helped shape it. Thanks to everyone who has been part of making it what it is.

About the Author

Nils Janse

Nils Janse is co-founder at Ymnig.ai, where he helps organizations adopt Gen AI through coaching, training, and an AI agent platform. With over a decade of entrepreneurial experience, he combines his engineering background (MSc from KTH and studies in AI) with management consulting expertise (formerly at McKinsey) to guide organizations through their Gen AI transformation journey. He has trained over 1,000 people in using Gen AI and worked with more than 60 companies on adopting Gen AI. Swedish viewers may recognize him from television appearances, including the SVT series "Generation AI". He lives in Stockholm with his fiancée and three kids.

About the Book

How can organizations adopt Generative AI and have AI coworkers multiply human capabilities?

Whether you're a leader driving Gen AI adoption, someone responsible for implementation, or anyone who wants to help shape how their organization works with AI, this book shows you how. Most organizations today know they need to do something about Gen AI, but they're struggling with exactly what and how. Some are stuck in excessive caution, while others have given people access to tools like ChatGPT but aren't seeing the impact they hoped for.

This guide shows you how to build an organization where humans and AI create unprecedented value together. Based on experience helping over 60 companies adopt Gen AI and coaching more than 1,000 people across teams, it walks you through the journey: understanding how Gen AI is rapidly evolving from AI chatbots to powerful AI coworkers, adopting Gen AI by augmenting people rather than just automating work, driving team-level adoption, and leading the broader transformation. You'll get practical guidance for everything from developing AI skills to implementing AI agents.

Written in accessible language and grounded in hands-on experience, this book is your roadmap for creating workplaces where AI truly multiplies human capabilities. It shows you how to build lasting organizational capabilities while capturing immediate value from Gen AI.

Made in the USA
Columbia, SC
13 April 2025